Routledge Revivals

Jewish Religious Conflicts

First published in 1950, *Jewish Religious Conflicts* gives an account of the principal cleavages that have taken place within the Jewish people since the close of the Old Testament over questions of religious faith, doctrine and practice. While passing in review the chief sects that have formed themselves during that period, it pays particular attention to the most recent cleavages, those between the 'orthodox' and 'reform', and between the 'conservative' and 'liberal' movements, which are dividing the Jewish community. This book will be of interest to students of religion and history.

Jewish Religious Conflicts

Maurice Simon

Routledge
Taylor & Francis Group

First published in 1950
By Hutchinson House

This edition first published in 2024 by Routledge
4 Park Square, Milton Park, Abingdon, Oxon, OX14 4RN
and by Routledge
605 Third Avenue, New York, NY 10017

Routledge is an imprint of the Taylor & Francis Group, an informa business

© Maurice Simon 1950

All rights reserved. No part of this book may be reprinted or reproduced or utilised in any form or by any electronic, mechanical, or other means, now known or hereafter invented, including photocopying and recording, or in any information storage or retrieval system, without permission in writing from the publishers.

Publisher's Note
The publisher has gone to great lengths to ensure the quality of this reprint but points out that some imperfections in the original copies may be apparent.

Disclaimer
The publisher has made every effort to trace copyright holders and welcomes correspondence from those they have been unable to contact.

A Library of Congress record exists under LCCN: 51009091

ISBN: 978-1-032-76245-6 (hbk)
ISBN: 978-1-003-47771-6 (ebk)
ISBN: 978-1-032-76246-3 (pbk)

Book DOI 10.4324/9781003477716

JEWISH RELIGIOUS CONFLICTS

by
MAURICE SIMON
M.A.

1950
HUTCHINSON'S UNIVERSITY LIBRARY
Hutchinson House, London, W.1

New York *Melbourne* *Sydney* *Cape Town*

THIS VOLUME IS NUMBER 48 IN
HUTCHINSON'S UNIVERSITY LIBRARY

*Printed in Great Britain
at the Gainsborough Press, St. Albans,
by Fisher, Knight and Co. Ltd.*

CONTENTS

		Page
Preface		7
Introduction: The Sources of *Torah*		9

PART ONE: THE HISTORIC SECTS

Chapter		
I	Judeans and Samaritans	17
II	Pharisees and Sadducees	26
III	Rabbis and Minim	38
IV	Rabbanites and Karaites	47
V	Maimunists and Anti-Maimunists	58
VI	Cabbalists and Anti-Cabbalists	68
VII	Chassidim and Mithnagedim	77

PART TWO: MODERN TRENDS

VIII	The Enlightenment Movement	89
IX	The Haskalah Movement	100
X	Emancipation and Jewish Law	111
XI	The Early Reform Movement and the Conservative Reaction	117
XII	The Advanced Reform Movement	127
XIII	Reform in America—The Mission of Israel	134
XIV	The Historical School	141
XV	Nationalist Judaism	149
	Glossary	163
	Bibliography	165
	Index	169

PREFACE

THE purpose of this work is to survey in a brief compass the chief internal religious conflicts which have agitated the Jewish people from the time of Ezra to the present day. Although throughout that period the Jewish people has always had a distinctive religion of its own, this religion has almost always existed under more than one form—that is to say, with more than one formulation of its vital principles—and while in the course of ages some forms have died out new ones have arisen to take their place. There are today numerous forms of Judaism, some of which differ more widely from one another than from certain other religions, but each of which proclaims itself to be the authentic form; and this phenomenon can be paralleled from some other stages of Jewish history. The growth of new forms has usually been accompanied by conflicts and controversies between those who supported and those who opposed them; and an account of these conflicts is perhaps the simplest means of bringing into relief the points at issue between the various parties and enabling the reader to distinguish the various forms.

The conflicts themselves fall into two well-marked divisions—an earlier and a later. The earlier comprises those conflicts which took place between the time of Ezra and that of Moses Mendelssohn towards the end of the eighteenth century. The latter comprises those which have been going on since the time of Mendelssohn. The earlier class are mainly of historic interest, being concerned with issues which can no longer be regarded as living. The latter are still active and closely affect the life of the individual Jew. The chief reason for combining the two in one survey is that the latter can hardly be understood without some knowledge of the former; and it is just this knowledge which the first part of this volume is intended to provide.

At the root of all the religious conflicts there has naturally lain the question? what precisely is the teaching of the Jewish religion? In so far as this teaching was held to originate in a divine revelation it was called in Hebrew *torah*, and was regarded as authoritative both for belief and for action. Up to quite recent times it was common ground among all Jews that the Pentateuch, the Five Books of Moses, was the fountain-head of *torah* and contained Jewish religious teaching in its most authoritative form. Whether any other books should be added to the Pentateuch as sources of *torah*, and if so with what degree of authority, was the question which more than any other led to conflicts and the formation of sects. Of recent times the authority and the revelational character of the Pentateuch itself have been impugned. The question of the sources of *torah*, if any, is thus intimately bound up with the subject of this work, and it recurs continually in the account of the various controversies. To elucidate it still further an introductory chapter has been inserted explaining more precisely what is meant by a "source of *torah*," and showing how the addition of new sources modified the character of the Jewish religion; also why the religion of *torah* derived from these sources was bound to create difficulties for the modernized Jews of the nineteenth century.

INTRODUCTION

THE SOURCES OF "TORAH"

THE Jewish people throughout the ages of its dispersion has been noted for its tenacious adherence to a religion of its own, known as the Jewish religion or Judaism. It is this religion which in the eyes of the world has chiefly distinguished it from other peoples. But in its own eyes what has chiefly distinguished it is not so much the religion as the possession of certain books from which the religion itself was derived by an intensive process of study and analysis. The subject-matter of these books in so far as it formed the source of the religion was called *torah*; and in treating of the Jewish religion it is necessary first to give some idea of the significance of this term for the Jewish people.

The word *torah* means literally guidance or instruction. As applied to religion it means divine guidance, guidance both of thought and of action which is supposed to have been derived directly or indirectly from a revelation. The Jewish people for many ages believed itself to be possessed of such a guidance through the instrumentality of certain books in which it was embodied; and on these books it based its religion.

The oldest of these books is the Pentateuch, the Five Books of Moses. This was the only source of *torah* in book form known to Ezra and his generation, by whom it was believed to have been transmitted to Moses through a direct revelation. On that account it has always been considered the book of *torah par excellence*. Before the Christian era a further source of guidance had been added in the shape of the Hebrew Scriptures. These like the Pentateuch were considered to be of divine origin, but to have been transmitted not by revelation but by inspiration. Later came books called the Talmud and the Midrashim (*vide* Chapter iii), which were not an original source but were themselves based on the Pentateuch and the Scriptures. They claimed only to make explicit what was implicit in these works, in virtue of a superior insight possessed by the Rabbis whose sayings they record. Finally the Talmud and Midrashim themselves, in conjunction with the Scriptures, became the basis of a Hebrew literature which threw their teaching into new and more modern forms. One of these midrashic works, the Zohar (*vide* Chapter vi) was of an exceptional character and was placed by many alongside the Talmud as a distinct source of *torah*.

By means of the prophetical works and the Talmud and Midrashim the scope of *torah* was greatly widened and matters were brought into its purview in which there had been no need to provide guidance in earlier times. The *torah* contained in the Pentateuch does not, explicitly, go beyond the ceremonial and social law of a somewhat primitive people. While this law remained from the days of Ezra the basis of the Jewish religion and the indispensable foundation of Jewish life, it ceased in the course of time to provide full satisfaction for the religious and spiritual needs of the Jewish people.

To meet these needs other elements were gradually introduced into the religion of which some hints indeed might be discovered in the Pentateuch, but the full warrant for which was provided only by the additional sources of *torah* which emerged later. Thus from the prophetical works the Jews derived a spiritual faith and uplift. The Talmud gave them on the one hand a juridical system, on the other hand an eschatology and a Messianic hope. The Bible on its purely literary side imbued them with a love of the Hebrew language for its own sake, which was also religious in character; and the Zohar was adopted by them as a text-book of Jewish mysticism.

All these elements—spirituality, eschatology, jurisprudence, Hebraism, and mysticism—are in themselves independent of the law of the Pentateuch, and it was the urge to add them to the law which was the ultimate cause of the emergence of new forms of *torah*, or of a new approach to the existing forms. Not all Jews felt this urge to the same degree, and it was this difference which led to religious conflicts and in some cases to the formation of distinct sects. In all cases, however, the new

INTRODUCTION: THE SOURCES OF "TORAH" 11

element gradually won the day and was eventually accepted by the majority as an integral part of the religion of *torah*. All these elements were embraced in the form of Judaism which was dominant in the eighteenth century, though the place of mysticism was still a matter of controversy.

Thus in the *torah* as embodied in its various text-books the Jews possessed a field of study sufficiently wide to absorb the whole of their intellectual energies. And in fact during long periods of their history, especially after the rise of Christianity, they studied practically nothing else. A conspicuous exception was the so-called Arabic period, from about the tenth to the thirteenth century, when they diligently studied Arabic literature (particularly its philosophical and scientific branches) in addition to their own *torah*. But after the decline of Arabic learning with the Christian conquest of Spain, the Jews began to fall back on their own *torah*, and for several centuries made little effort to add to it any knowledge from outside sources.

During all this period the influence of the *torah* on the Jewish life and conduct was paramount. It was exercised, of course, chiefly through their religion, and it led them to form religious communities possessing a strong organic cohesion and sharply distinguished from their non-Jewish surroundings. Thus organized the Jews stood in a separate relation from the rest of the inhabitants to the secular authorities and lived their own life, seeking no more than a minimum of contact with their non-Jewish surroundings.

At no time perhaps was the *torah* more dominant in Jewish life than at the beginning of the eighteenth century, and at no time perhaps was the Jewish people as a whole more absorbed in itself and indifferent to the life of its environment. About the middle of that century, however, a new spirit began to manifest itself among them. It was about that time that the Christian Church finally lost in the most advanced countries of Western Europe, especially England, France and Germany, the dominance which it had long exercised over both intellectual and social life. In the intellectual field the human reason had vindicated its right to be considered the final arbiter on all questions of truth and untruth to which it could be applied. In the social field the State had substituted itself for the Church as the supreme organization of human society. A new era which may be called the modern age had commenced in western Europe.

This development was not unobserved by the Jews, and it led to the emergence among them of a new spirit which may be designated "modern," and which for the purposes of this work may be defined as a desire to participate on the one hand in the intellectual movement, and on the other hand in the social evolution, of the modern world. They were impelled to partake in the former by their innate mental alertness and restlessness, fostered as it was by certain features in their own literature; and they sought to profit from the latter in order to improve their own material position. The former endeavour found expression in a striving for enlightenment or modern knowledge, the latter in a striving for emancipation or the removal of civil disabilities and the acquisition of full civic rights.

In the nineteenth century the "modernism" of the eighteenth century was itself rendered old-fashioned by the further progress of knowledge and invention in Western Europe. With the use of more exact methods and instruments, "rational inquiry" was replaced by "scientific research"; and as a result chiefly of historical investigation, the concept of the "nation" was separated from that of the "state," and given an importance of its own. Jews sought to keep abreast of these developments also; they cultivated a scientific outlook and habit of mind, and based their social relations on a Jewish national self-consciousness.

In these endeavours to modernize themselves the Jews were hampered not a little by the *torah* and the religion which they had inherited from the past, and the whole tendency of which was to keep them isolated from their surroundings. The easiest course to follow for Jews who were influenced by the "modern spirit" was to throw off their religion and cease to be Jews; and this was the course actually taken by many. The majority of them, however, were loth to discard their Judaism, and they sought to effect some accommodation between it and the modern spirit by circumscribing the influence of *torah* over their lives and by omitting those features of the religion which

INTRODUCTION: THE SOURCES OF "TORAH" 13

were not in harmony with the new ideas and emphasizing those which were. In this way new forms of Judaism arose corresponding to the main trends in the modern spirit, which may be designated broadly the Judaism of enlightenment, the Judaism of emancipation, the Judaism of research, and the Judaism of nationalism; and within these again there were various subdivisions according to the way in which the accommodation was made and the emphasis which was placed respectively on the old or the new.

It is the chief purpose of this book to describe these various forms and explain how they arose, and their relation to one another and to the parent form which preceded them and continued to exist side by side with them. This form may be called Rabbinic Judaism because it was dominated by the *torah* teaching of the Jewish scholars of the early Christian centuries commonly known as "the Rabbis."

Thus, in the nineteenth century, the uniformity which Judaism exhibited in the eighteenth was broken up. This disintegration first affected the Jews of Western Europe and America, but afterwards it spread also to those of the Russian Empire, which contained more than half of the Jews of the world. Here, living under medieval conditions, the bulk of the Jews clung to the old form of the religion, and towards the end of the century, when they commenced to emigrate *en masse* to Western countries, they brought about a revival of it in England and America as well. Hence this form of Judaism— which may be called Rabbinic on account of its scrupulous adherence to the teaching of the Rabbis of the early Christian centuries—remained the dominant form throughout the nineteenth century, and all the other forms, which sought to take account of the spirit of the age, might be regarded as secessions from it or revolts against it.

The upheavals which have taken place in Eastern Europe in the present century have, however, caused its virtual disappearance in the regions which were for centuries, and especially in the nineteenth century, its chief stronghold. It is now trying desperately hard to create—or recreate—for itself a home and a centre in Palestine, the land of its origin. This it is attempting to do under the aegis not of a Temple, as in the old days, but, strangely enough, of an ultra-modern form of Judaism which stands at the opposite pole of Jewish sentiment and outlook.

How this strange alliance has been brought about it is not the purpose of the present work to inquire; but the succeeding pages may help to explain how the two forms differ in their basic conceptions and how nevertheless the term Judaism may be used to cover both.

PART I
THE HISTORIC SECTS

CHAPTER I

JUDEANS AND SAMARITANS

THE first great religious conflict within the Jewish people—once Judaism had become definitely the religion of *torah* with monotheism as its basic doctrine—arose over the question whether its "sacred book" should be the Pentateuch only or should include also a number of other writings, those which along with the Pentateuch form what is now called the "Old Testament." The Pentateuch contains a law—ceremonial, social and moral—the other books contain no law; and in all ages there have been Jews who regarded the law as the be-all and end-all of their religion and thought little of its other elements.

An attempt to base a monotheistic Jewish religion on the Pentateuch alone was made at an early period after the Exile by the sect known to us as Samaritans. The bulk of the Jewish people, on the other hand, then known as Judeans, added a number of other writings to the Pentateuch to form their "sacred book." By doing so they paved the way for Rabbinic Judaism, for the proper understanding of which therefore it is necessary to consider why they took this course, and how through doing so they gave their religion a different stamp from that of the Samaritans.

When Ezra the priest came from Babylon to Jerusalem his object was, as he tells us, "to teach in Israel statutes and ordinances."[1] His chief instrument for this purpose was the Mosaic legislation contained in the Pentateuch. Now that legislation occupies considerably less than half of the Pentateuch. It could easily be reduced to the form of a code and presented as a separate work. It would have been natural for Ezra to draw up such a code, and perhaps for practical purposes

[1] Ezra, vii, 10.

he did so virtually, if not actually. Formally, however, he presented the code as part of the whole Pentateuch, of which he was a "ready scribe."[1] Obviously therefore he attached to the rest of the Pentateuch a value little if at all less than to the code itself.

What the nature of this value was becomes clear from a consideration of certain incidents related in the book of Nehemiah. We are there told that after the walls of Jerusalem had been completed the whole people assembled in the great square of the city and Ezra the priest read to them out of the book of the *torah* of Moses from early morning until midday; also that the Levites "caused the people to understand the law."[2] And on a later occasion on a day of fasting and repentance, "they read in the book of the Law a fourth part of the day, and another fourth part they confessed and prostrated themselves before the Lord their God."[3]

Now it can hardly be supposed that so much time on such occasions would be taken up with reading only the legal parts of the Pentateuch. We may well surmise that some if not all of the sections read were chosen for their edificatory or homiletical value, that is, in this case, for creating in the hearers the right mood or frame of mind for acknowledging the unity of God and performing the precepts.

Certain it is that the Scribes who followed Ezra and who for several generations continued his work of "teaching statutes and ordinances in Israel" attached to the non-legal part of the Pentateuch this edificatory or homiletical value. Nor were they content with the Pentateuch alone for this purpose. There were already current in the time of Ezra a number of Hebrew books which were generally considered to have been composed under the influence of what was called "the holy spirit," and the authorship of which was attributed for the most part to prophets who had arisen in Israel from the time of Joshua onwards. In the view of the Scribes these books, or some of them, possessed an edificatory or homiletical value little inferior to that of the Pentateuch, and they therefore copied and disseminated them as they did the Pentateuch, no doubt editing and revising them at the same time, so as to make them as

[1] Ezra, vii, 6. [2] Neh. viii, 7. [3] Ib. ix, 3.

suitable as possible for their purpose. They even added books composed later, like the Book of Ezra itself. In this way there was gradually built up a sacred literature, the text and arrangement of which were standardized some time before the commencement of the Christian era, and to which was given the general name of *mikra* ("reading," or "reading matter").

The action of the Scribes in enlarging the *mikra* by adding to the Pentateuch the writings of prophets subsequent to Moses led to a sharp conflict between the Judeans and another branch of the Israelitish people which also professed a strict adherence to the Mosaic religion. These were the Samaritans, the people who inhabited Samaria and the neighbouring district after the downfall of the Northern Kingdom of Israel. They consisted partly of the remnants of the Israelitish population, partly of an admixture of foreign elements brought in by the Assyrian kings. For some centuries they were heathens, though they seem to have adopted a number of Jewish practices, including sacrifice to the God of Israel. In spite of this an offer made by them to co-operate in the building of the Second Temple was decisively rejected by the Judeans. From this time they carried on with the Judeans a bitter feud which was more or less a continuation both in the religious and the political spheres of the feud between the Northern and Southern kingdoms in pre-exilic days. They were later converted to a genuine form of Judaism apparently by a priest named Manasseh who, shortly before or after the death of Ezra, took refuge with them when he was deposed from his priesthood in Jerusalem for having married a non-Jewish wife. Whether under the influence of Manasseh or in some other way they became strict monotheists, and accepted the Pentateuch as their code of law.

In two respects, however, the Samaritans followed a different line from the Judeans. One was that they refused to recognize as sacred any book besides the Pentateuch; in other words, they denied the validity of any prophecy save that of Moses. The other was that they regarded as the proper spot for the sanctuary not Jerusalem but Mount Gerizim, a place in their own territory, on which they actually raised one in the time of Alexander the Great. They even at some time or other interpolated into the Pentateuch a number of passages in which the holiness of Mount Gerizim was clearly stated. The reason for their insistence on this point seems to have been primarily political. They claimed to be the successors of the Northern Kingdom, to which the name of Israel properly applied. They therefore resented any attempt of the Judeans to make Jerusalem the religious centre of Judaism. And it was no doubt this claim, as well as the fact that their origins went back to a period before the Jews had accepted the prophetical canon, which led them to reject the prophets who came after Moses.

Closely connected with the Judean claim for the supremacy of Jerusalem was that of the inalienable right of the house of the Judean David to the kingship of Israel. The Samaritans, as heirs of the Northern Kingdom, were, of course, unwilling to admit this claim also, and it thus became impossible for them to admit the validity of post-Mosaic prophecy.

Whatever may have been the motives of the Samaritans for this course—and the scantiness of our information about them does not enable us to speak with certainty on the point—we can discern clearly enough its religious effects. For one thing it led the Samaritans, in spite of their following the same law as the Judeans, to adopt a way of life widely differing in many respects. Not being subject to the authority of the teachers in Jerusalem, they carried out the laws in their own fashion, which often diverged considerably from that of the Judeans. In particular, they fixed the degrees of consanguinity within which marriage was prohibited differently from the Judeans, and the latter in consequence refused to intermarry with them and would not regard them as members of the same community.

In addition to this practical difference, there was also a deep spiritual difference between the Samaritans and the Judeans, due to the acceptance by the latter of the *mikra*. Like the Judeans, the Samaritans recognized the kingship of God. But they derived their idea of that kingship solely from the law, and therefore could conceive of it in relation to Israel only. In other words their religion was purely particularistic. Now the religion of the Judeans, being centred in the law, was also, of course, basically particularistic. But the *mikra* revealed to them a concept of God as king not only of Israel but of the whole earth, and so added a universalistic side to their religion. This was the first broadening of the original religion of *torah* as propounded by Ezra, and the first step in its metamorphosis into the Rabbinism of later generations.

Apart from this it may be said that the Judeans accepted the *mikra* because in general they wanted to *think* about their religion, and the Samaritans rejected it because they did not. To the Samaritans religion was essentially a matter of routine performance in which the mind had little part. It was a "commandment of man instilled into them," to be carried out mechanically without being correlated with the rest of their lives. Its observance rested on a sense of discipline, not on any personal or living interest in it. This sense of discipline was likely to be weakened rather than strengthened by the study of the *mikra*, and no doubt this was the fundamental reason why the Samaritans eschewed such study.

The Judeans also entertained a profound respect for their teachers, as represented by the priests and scribes, and these in turn followed scrupulously the traditions handed down to them from previous generations. Nevertheless, while willing and anxious to carry out the commandments, they were at the same time desirous to have some idea why they were called upon to observe them and what benefit the observance would bring them. Answers to these questions are, of course, to be found in the Pentateuch itself. But these answers applied directly to a time long past, when conditions were very different from those of the post-exilic period. Revised or additional answers were required based on the experience through which the people of Israel had passed during the intervening centuries.

These answers were to be found in the other books of the *mikra*, or at any rate in the Pentateuch read in conjunction with them; for the study of them stimulated interest in the Pentateuch itself. A *mikra* which was confined to the Pentateuch was in effect no *mikra*; only when supplemented by the *mikra* of the other books could it give the inspiration of which the Judeans felt the need but to which the Samaritans were indifferent.

The Scribes, and the Rabbis who followed them, so far agreed with the Samaritans as to draw a rather sharp distinction between the sacredness of the Pentateuch and that of the rest of the Scriptures—similar to that drawn in the Tabernacle or Temple between the "holy of holies" and the mere "holy." The addition to the Pentateuch of the other books did not mean that these occupied the same place in the religion of *torah*. The title of *torah* was reserved usually for the five Books of Moses (sometimes even specifically for their legal portions), the main purpose of which was to provide a rule for action. The primary purpose of the *mikra*, on the other hand, as we have seen, was to encourage and stimulate the Jews to think about their religion, while keeping thought within channels which would not be dangerous to religion.

This does not necessarily mean that the books comprised in the *mikra* were originally composed for this purpose, or even that they were left in their original form. But there can be little doubt that the Scribes hall-marked them, so to speak, as *mikra* primarily in order that they might serve this purpose. A striking instance of this process is afforded by the dictum of Rabbi Akiba, the great Rabbinical authority of the first half of the second century C.E.: "All the Scriptural books are holy, but the Song of Songs is holy of holies." The Song of Songs, as might be expected from the nature of its contents, was one of the books which had to fight hardest for its inclusion, or retention, in the canon. Rabbi Akiba, discerning the great spiritual value which might be imparted to it by an allegorical interpretation, insisted that it should be retained, naturally with this qualification; and his opinion was decisive.

Generally speaking, however, it is not easy for us to say what precisely were the criteria applied by the Scribes. While their primary object was undoubtedly edification, they seem by no means to have been insensible to literary values as such, and they appear to have included some books largely on this ground. Why they drew the line exactly where they did must always remain something of a mystery to us, especially seeing that the Scribes in Alexandria who translated the Scriptures into Greek drew the line somewhat differently. However, the exclusion of two or three of the more doubtful books from the Hebrew

JUDEANS AND SAMARITANS 23

Scriptures or the inclusion of a few from the Greek canon would not materially affect the character of the *mikra*, which is fixed chiefly by the Pentateuch and the prophetical works. These are sufficient to establish its value for purposes of edification.

The attitude of Rabbinic Judaism to the *mikra* is perhaps best revealed in a saying of Rabbi Ada bar Chaninah, an authority of the fourth century of the Christian era: "Had Israel not sinned, they would have had only the Pentateuch and the Book of Joshua."[1] The thought underlying this remark seems to be that after their settlement in the Land of Canaan the Israelites fell from the high spiritual level to which they had been raised by Moses and Joshua, and required an additional instrument to bring them back to it. This instrument was provided by the *mikra*, the function of which is thus to establish a communion between the individual and God similar to that which was originally created between the whole community and God by their collective obedience to the law. At the same time these words of R. Ada seem to contain an oblique stricture on the Samaritans for presuming to think that they could dispense with this instrument and for ignoring the national legacy of sin.

By accepting the *mikra* the Judeans showed a superiority in intelligence over the Samaritans, and at the same time they acquired an instrument for developing that superiority. Writing at the beginning of the second century B.C., the Judean Joshua ben Sirach could speak of "the stupid people that dwell in Samaria," and this feeling of contempt seems to have been embedded in the very name which the Judeans gave the Samaritans—Cutheans, or men of Cuth, a heathen city beyond the Euphrates.

Certainly in attempting to preserve the Mosaic religion without the *mikra* the Samaritans stunted their spiritual growth and condemned themselves more or less to intellectual stagnation. Nevertheless their steadfast adherence to that religion as they understood it through many generations commands a certain respect. The Rabbis discussed the question whether the Samaritans were to be regarded as what they called

[1] *Nedarim* 22b.

"proselytes of lions"[1] or "proselytes of righteousness," that is to say, whether their Judaism was a mere superstition and devil-worship, or whether it was based on a genuine faith. The Rabbis inclined to the latter opinion, and this is on the whole confirmed by a survey of Samaritan history and literature.

The Temple which the Samaritans built on Mount Gerizim in the time of Alexander was destroyed by the Judean king John Hyrcanus in 132 B.C., and from that time they ceased to be a menace to the Judeans either as a political or a religious force. They continued, however, to regard Gerizim as their holy mountain and to bring sacrifices on it, and they retained the institution of a high priesthood. Their numbers for a long time remained considerable, and while their headquarters were always in the district of Samaria they had settlements in Damascus and other places. Their attachment to the *torah* as they understood it was so strong that a Jewish Rabbi once remarked that the Samaritans were more particular than the Jews themselves in the observance of those precepts which they had adopted. Like the Judeans they refused to make any compromise with paganism, and equally with them they rejected the worship of Jesus. They also sided with the Jews at a later date in declining to exchange the *torah* for the Koran, though in course of time they came to accept from the Arabs a number of practices and beliefs which gave their religion a Mohammedan tinge.

After the suppression of the revolt of the Jews under Bar Cochba in 135 C.E., the Romans allowed the Samaritans, who had assisted them, to rebuild their Temple on Mount Gerizim. This also, however, was destroyed by the Christians in 484, and from about that period the Samaritan community began to decline, till today there are only a handful of them left, in the neighbourhood of Nablous. Their period of greatest literary activity was in the fourteenth century, when they produced a number of liturgical and apologetic works.

---

[1] This expression is based on the statement in 2. Kings xvii, 24 *sqq.*, that the men whom the king of Assyria brought from Babylon and other places to Samaria at first "feared not the Lord, wherefore the Lord sent lions among them which killed some of them," and that thereupon the king of Assyria sent to them a priest who "taught them how they should fear the Lord."

Like the Judeans, and perhaps in imitation of them, the Samaritans developed an eschatology, of which the essential feature was the advent at the end of days of a divine deliverer called Taheb (perhaps="one who returns" or "brings back"). Characteristically enough, the Taheb was to be not a scion of the House of David, like the Jewish Messiah, but a prophet of the type of Moses, who would restore the period of grace with the Tabernacle and worship on Mount Gerizim, as well as the temporal prosperity of the nation.

Within the Samaritan fold itself a somewhat original line was taken by a certain Dositheus, of whom, under the name of Dostai, mention is made in Rabbinical sources also. As far as can be gathered from the scanty references to him available, he lived in the first century of the Christian era, and was held in high esteem by his fellow-Samaritans, who regarded him as a precursor of the Taheb. At the same time he seems to have been on good terms with the Rabbinical authorities, from whom he adopted many practices and interpretations of the Bible. His followers were called Dositheans, and they still had synagogues in Sichem in the ninth century.[1]

[1] It is possible that the Hebrew fragment discovered some years ago of which a translation is given in Charles, Apocrypha and Pseudo-epigrapha of the Old Testament, II, 785-814, is Dosithean, though in its general character it is more Sadducean than Samaritan. The hoard of Hebrew MSS. recently discovered near the Dead Sea contains fragments which show a certain affinity to this one, and render it probable that it formed part of the religious literature of Jewish sectaries of the Herodian period.

CHAPTER II

PHARISEES AND SADDUCEES

THE conflict between the Samaritans and the Judeans was followed at no long interval by one of no less historical and religious importance within the Judean community itself. The fundamental question at issue in this conflict, on the religious side, was whether the spiritual leader of the people should be the priest or the teacher; and in their endeavours to establish their position the teachers laid the foundations of the work which became subsequently the great pillar of Rabbinic Judaism, the Talmud.

The Mosaic legislation as set forth in the Pentateuch falls into two well-defined sections. One consists of the regulations for the service in the sanctuary (called in Hebrew *abodah*, or service). These were the special, though not the exclusive concern of the priests, who alone were qualified to minister in the sanctuary. The other section consists of regulations applying to the whole of the people, priests and laymen alike. This may further be divided into the regulations for the judges and other officers who had to administer as well as keep the law, and those for the mass of the people, who had only to keep it.

From the time of Ezra to that of the Maccabees the heads of the Jewish community in Palestine were High Priests whose first function was to minister in the sanctuary and supervise the other priests. Ezra himself was a priest, and he might naturally have been expected to be more concerned for the strict performance of the Temple service by his fellow-priests than for the observance of the law in general. Actually, however, he made it his chief concern not to watch over the Temple service but to "teach law and ordinance in Israel." In other words, he placed the general observance of the law—the *torah*

—at least on a par with the priestly performance of the *abodah* or Temple service.

We have striking evidence that this policy was adhered to by Ezra's successors in the priesthood up to the time of the Maccabees. Most distinguished among the High Priests of this period were two named Simon, one or both of whom were surnamed "the Just," and of whom the earlier functioned in the time of Alexander the Great, the later about a century afterwards. To one or other of these is attributed the saying: "By three things is the world [i.e., specifically the Jewish people] upheld, by the *torah* [the Mosaic legislation in general], by the *abodah* [the Temple service], and by *gemiluth hasadim* (lit. "performance of kindnesses," i.e., acts prompted by love of neighbour)." It is highly significant that such an authority should place *torah* before *abodah*.

A different view was taken by the High Priests of the Hasmonean House, who from the time of Simon, the brother of Judas Maccabeus (142–135 B.C.), stood at the head of the state of Judea. Their policy was in the main one of national aggrandizement. Like their predecessors in the high priesthood, they punctiliously maintained the Temple service, taking their own due part in it when required by the law. But they seem to have been indifferent to the observance of the law by the people in general. They placed *abodah* before *torah*, and left *gemiluth hasadim* entirely out of account. They were anxious to make Israel a powerful rather than a righteous nation, and took no interest in the dissemination of religious knowledge.

In this policy they were zealously seconded by a party called Zadokites, or in the Greek form of the name, Sadducees, which became prominent in the latter part of the second century B.C. The origin of the name Zadokites is uncertain; it would naturally mean "followers or descendants of Zadok," but if so, this Zadok cannot be identified with certainty. The Saducean party consisted chiefly of members of the leading priestly families (of whom that of Zadok was probably one). With them were associated a number of prominent and influential laymen; and between them they monopolized the chief offices of state, including the administration of justice.

To the Sadducees the Mosaic legislation was essentially a state law, the chief object of which was to preserve the unity of the nation and so make it strong. They observed it themselves and called on others to observe it just in so far as was necessary for this purpose. Like the Samaritans, they were attached to the *torah* not so much by inner conviction as by a strong sense of discipline and loyalty, combined in their case with a powerful vested interest.

In marked contrast to the attitude of the Sadducees to the *torah* was that of a rival group known as Pharisees, a name of which also the origin is uncertain. Whether as a reaction against the conduct of the Sadducees or for some other reason, this group made it their deliberate object to emphasize the claims of the law in general against those of the Temple service in particular. Not that they in any way disparaged or neglected the latter; but they paid particular attention to those precepts which were incumbent on them as laymen, seeking by all means to avoid the least suspicion of transgression.

For this purpose they were especially careful in putting aside from all produce the portions due to the priests and levites, and refrained from partaking of any food from which they were not certain that such dues had been removed. They applied the same meticulous care to the performance of other precepts also, especially those relating to levitical cleanliness and uncleanness. They thus formed a class apart, and this was certainly one reason, if not the original one, why they were known as *Perushim* (lit. "separate").

The significance of the Pharisees for Jewish religious development was due chiefly to their close association with the Scribes. By this time the Scribes had almost completed their work of establishing the canon, and had transferred their principal activity to another field. It had always been part of their task to carry on the work of Ezra in "teaching law and ordinance in Israel," but they now commenced to widen the scope and extent of this work out of all recognition. To Ezra and his immediate successors "law and ordinance" in this connection must have meant simply the precepts written down in the Pentateuch with a few necessary explanations. To the Scribes of the Hasmonean period it meant in addition a host of other rules and precepts the knowledge of which they were equally anxious to disseminate among the people.

These additional rules and precepts bore in the main to those of the Pentateuch the relation of regulations to statutes. Their chief object was to bring the laws of the Pentateuch—which were in general drawn in wide terms—into closer touch with practical life. They extended the laws of the Pentateuch from the general to the particular, showing how they were to be applied in detail—often in very minute detail—to the conduct of the individual. The instructions of the Scribes were supposed to represent the custom of the people of Israel from the time of Moses, or at any rate of the prophets, and therefore to possess a validity and authority on a par with that of the Pentateuch itself. There was no written record of them, but the Scribes claimed to be their authentic depositaries and expounders, in virtue of an unbroken tradition going back to Moses himself. They had not yet been reduced to fixed form, but they were numerous enough and comprehensive enough to form a body of Jewish law collateral with that of the Pentateuch.

This body of law was also regarded by the Scribes as *torah*, or part of the divine revelation, but in view of its somewhat ancillary character it was never put into writing, and therefore came to be known—and was perhaps already known at this time—as *torah she-be'al-peh* (lit. "*torah* by word of mouth*,*" or Oral Law), in contradistinction to the *torah she-biktab* ("*torah* in writing") or Written Law of the Pentateuch.

The Sadducees, as might have been expected, rejected the claim of the Scribes to put the Oral Law on the same level as the Written. While they must often for practical purposes have adopted the regulations of the Oral Law, they did not regard them as binding. Seeking as they did to retain the administration of the law in their own hands, they found it to their advantage to keep it as elastic as possible, and were naturally averse to having their hands tied by a multiplicity of detailed regulations. For the same reason they were opposed to the whole educational activity of the Scribes. If they could not prevent the mass of the people from knowing the Pentateuch, they were not anxious for them to busy themselves too much with matters of religion.

To the Pharisees, on the other hand, obsessed as they were with the pursuit of righteousness, the Oral Law was precious. It promised to give them exactly what they wanted—a religious rule or regulation for every occasion of life. They therefore accepted in their entirety the claims of the Scribes on behalf of the binding character of the Oral Law, as an integral part of the religion of *torah*, co-ordinate with the Written Law, and they followed it wherever possible, even where it seemed to depart from the literal meaning of the text. This procedure led to certain marked differences in religious practice between them and the Sadducees. But what chiefly distinguished them was that they set the highest possible value on the knowledge of the Oral Law, and therefore looked up to the Scribes as their spiritual guides.

Closely connected with this difference in practice and outlook between the Pharisees and Sadducees was one in theological belief and dogma. The Pharisees believed fervently in the coming of a "day of the Lord," when God would judge all mankind, both the living and the dead, and deal with them according to their deserts, rewarding the righteous and punishing the wicked. This belief was based on certain apocalyptic visions of "the Day of the Lord" contained in the Hebrew Scriptures, notably that of the "end of days" in Daniel xii, which probably provided inspiration to Mattathias the Hasmonean and his followers in their revolt against the Syrian king, and may indeed have been written at this time. It added, however, one feature of cardinal importance. At the "end of days"—which might be near or far off but seems usually to have been thought of as being not very distant—the kingship of Israel would be miraculously restored to a scion of the House of David, called the Messiah (i.e., "anointed one"), and his throne would be established in righteousness, heralding the approach of the last judgment and the resurrection.

The Sadducees, if they did not entirely reject this belief, at least treated it with scepticism. They could find no mention of it in the law, and the references to it in the other biblical books did not carry sufficient weight with them to establish a

PHARISEES AND SADDUCEES 31

dogma. Like the Oral Law, the belief in the resurrection remained a badge of Pharisaism, and by it was transmitted to subsequent types of Judaism.

Pharisaism thus had three distinguishing marks—the observance of levitical purity by laymen, the acceptance of the Oral Law, and the belief in the Messianic age, the last judgment and the resurrection. At first sight it is not easy to see any inherent connection between these characteristics, nor do the scanty records of Pharisaism which have come down to us enable us to establish one with certainty. Yet it is natural to suppose that all three were the product of the same religious outlook or purpose, nor is it difficult to surmise what this may have been.

Strongly as they were attached to the Temple service, the Pharisees were well aware that it was not fulfilling the function originally contemplated for it in the Mosaic legislation. The first command to erect a sanctuary was contained in the words of God to Moses: "Speak unto the children of Israel . . . that they make Me a sanctuary and I shall dwell in their midst."[1] This was interpreted to mean that the highest purpose of the sanctuary was to bring down the Divine Presence, the *Shekhinah* (lit. "abiding") from heaven to earth, so as to constitute in some way a link between the two. According to the belief of the Jews in the time of the Pharisees, this condition had been fulfilled both in the Tabernacle of the wilderness and in the first Temple. But they were under no illusion that the *Shekhinah* was present in the Second Temple. It could not be thought, therefore, that the *abodah* there, however faithfully performed, was accomplishing its highest purpose.

It is possible to explain all the three peculiarities of the Pharisees as deliberate attempts to remedy this deficiency. First, as to the levitical purity. The absence of the Divine Presence from the sanctuary may well have led to a certain slackness and negligence among the priests, such as was actually complained of by the prophet Malachi. It may be, therefore, that the Pharisees thought to keep the priests and Levites up to the mark by themselves performing even more than they were required in the matter of levitical purity.

[1] Exodus xxv, 8.

Again, if the Divine Presence was not in the Temple, it could not be supposed that the sacrifices which they themselves brought produced their object in being a "sweet savour to the Lord." They therefore may have thought to make amends by their punctilious observance not only of the Written but also of the Oral Law. Lastly, the Divine Presence over the Temple had in former times been the sign of God's kingship on earth. Since this sign was absent they had to replace it by a belief which made that kingship at least present to their minds.

The eschatological beliefs of the Pharisees were embodied in a number of works written in the last two or three centuries of the Second Temple, partly in Hebrew, partly in Aramaic and partly in Greek, and containing an apocalyptic vision of the "end of days." They were all pseudepigraphic, the authorship being assigned to some ancient worthy like Enoch or Moses or Isaiah. The chief of those originally written in Hebrew are the First Book of Enoch, the Book of Jubilees, the Testaments of the Twelve Patriarchs, and the Assumption of Moses. None of them, however, has come down to us in the Hebrew original, and we know them only from Greek and other translations.[1]

Their attitude to the law often differed somewhat from that of the Scribes, and it was for that reason probably that the Scribes did not trouble to copy and preserve them. Their eschatological doctrines were, however, on the whole, if not fully, in accord with the beliefs of the Scribes and the Pharisees, and through their agency became an integral part of Rabbinic Judaism, though their literary source was completely forgotten by the Rabbinic Jews themselves.

At some time which we cannot exactly determine, but which was probably in the Hasmonean period, the Scribes as such (i.e., as copyists proper) ceased to be the authoritative expounders of the law and were replaced in the performance of this function by men known as *Chakhamim* ("wise men," sing. *chakham*). The *Chakhamim*, like the Scribes, had an

---

[1] The recently discovered Dead Sea manuscript hoard has, however, brought to light the Hebrew text of some hitherto unknown works of this nature.

intimate knowledge of the traditions connected with the *torah*, though they reckoned themselves as inferior to the earlier Scribes and as bound by all the decisions which the Scribes had taken. The Pharisees transferred their allegiance to the *Chakhamim* and encouraged them to continue the work of the Scribes in the development of the Oral Law. It was these *Chakhamim* who completed the process commenced by the Scribes of making the teachers of the Oral Law the spiritual leaders of the Jewish people. This they did chiefly by embodying and fixing the Oral Law in the form called *halakhah*, a term of capital importance in the scheme of Rabbinic Judaism.

The word *halakhah* means literally "going about," "walking." It was applied—apparently from the time of the Scribes—to the right way of carrying out any given precept of the Pentateuch. It was, in fact, the rule laid down by the Oral Law, as distinct from the Written, for action in any given circumstances. It would seem that in the time of the early Scribes very few if any of these rules had been actually formulated. But there existed already a vast mass of precedents and decisions which provided the material for their formulation and which could serve as a basis for fresh precedents and decisions.

The first attempts to formulate such rules took the shape of glosses attached to the text of the Scripture, as part and parcel of its interpretation. When Ezra "taught law and ordinance in Israel," we must suppose that he attached to each *mitzvah* (precept) in the Pentateuch some explanation of the way in which it should be carried out. The oldest commentaries which we possess on the Bible, the so-called *Mekhilta*, *Sifre* and *Sifra* on the legal parts of the Pentateuch, some elements of which probably go back to the time of the Scribes, are of this nature. Thus on the rule laid down in Leviticus i, 4 that one who brings a burnt-offering shall lay his hands on it, the *Sifre* comments that Israelites lay their hands but not Gentiles, that males lay hands but not females. Such rules came themselves to be called *halakhoth*, and represent the first attempt to give the Oral Law fixed shape and form.

In course of time these rules were separated from the text of the Scripture and presented in an independent form, each rule being known by the name of an *halakhah*. But the rules of the Oral Law which could be attached to a text of the Scripture were only a comparatively small part of the total number. In addition there were those which were derived from the Scripture by a somewhat roundabout and even arbitrary process called *midrash* or "inquiry," of which the Sages alone possessed the secret, and those which derived their validity simply from ancient custom and tradition. Gradually these also were cast into the form of *halakhah*, i.e., short pithy formulas calculated to provide the guidance which was most needed in practice for the observance of the law. Thus the Oral Law came to consist of *halakhoth* in the same way as the Written Law consisted of *mitzvoth*.

Who originated this process we do not know, but it certainly received its chief development from two teachers who lived in Jerusalem in the time of Herod the Great (30 B.C.– A.D. 4). Their names were Hillel and Shammai, and they were the real founders of Rabbinic Judaism. They made it their business to collect, sift and arrange the *halakhahs* which had already been accumulated and to extend their number so as to cover the whole range of the Oral Law.

In their hands the Oral Law began to take shape as a definite system of law which could be methodically studied and applied. They gave it the outlines of a book which, though still transmitted orally, was already capable of being written down, and which definitely saved it from the danger of being forgotten. They still left much to be done before the collected *halakhahs* could be regarded as complete, but they laid a foundation on which their successors could build and did build.

It was Hillel and Shammai who first concentrated the chief attention of the Jewish religious teachers on the Oral Law, and gave it a status, for purposes of reference, independent of the Written Law. It was their object to frame *halakhahs* in such a way that they should provide the religious teacher (or the Rabbi, as he came to be called) with a clue which would enable him to answer any question put to him in the field of Jewish religious law. These questions fell almost entirely into the four following categories, which between them covered practically the whole field of Jewish life:

PHARISEES AND SADDUCEES

(1) whether any given action was permitted or forbidden;
(2) whether any given individual or group was liable to or exempt from any specified obligation;
(3) whether any given living or inanimate object was or was not a fit instrument with which to perform a certain specified religious duty;
(4) whether any given person or chattel was in certain circumstances ritually clean or unclean.

For answering these questions the Scribes had resorted in the first instance to the Written Law. Hillel and Shammai made it the practice to resort in the first instance to the *halakhah*. The superiority of this method for practical purposes was obvious, and the teachers of the *torah* did not rest until they had digested the whole of the Oral Law into a systematic and well arranged collection of *halakhoth*.

At an early period it became customary to call any group of *halakhoth* dealing with a single subject a *mishnah* (lit. "repetition," because they were meant to be repeated and meditated on). Various Rabbis had each his own particular *mishnah*, on which he more or less specialized. Gradually the various *mishnahs* coalesced and formed a book. The first versions of this book were made before the middle of the second century A.D., but the final and definitive version was that produced about the year 180 by Rabbi Judah, surnamed Ha-Nasi (the Prince). This book became known as the Mishnah, *par excellence*, and has ever since ranked along with the Scriptures as one of the "sacred books" of Rabbinic Judaism. For some generations, however, it probably continued to be transmitted orally.

With the decline of the Hasmonean house after the entry of the Roman general Pompey into Jerusalem in 63 B.C., both the Sadducees and the Pharisees lost their political importance and became purely religious sects. While retaining their old religious differences with regard to the Oral Law and the Last Judgment, they found a new subject of dispute in the question of the immortality of the soul, which now apparently for the first time began to engage seriously the attention of the Jews of Palestine. The latter probably had learnt to distinguish clearly the soul from the body from the Greek-speaking Jews of Alexandria, who had themselves no doubt learnt it from the Greeks.

The idea that the soul survived the body fitted in well with the importance which the Pharisees attached to the individual, and it was therefore natural for them to accept it. In order, however, to adapt it better to their notions of the Last Judgment they gave it a new turn, which was apparently foreign to the Alexandrian Jews, by introducing the doctrine of reincarnation at the end of days and the physical resurrection at any rate of the righteous. The doctrine of reincarnation was naturally rejected uncompromisingly by the Sadducees, but on the question of the soul's survival they seem to have been divided. Even those who accepted this belief, however, seem still to have rejected the notion of reward and punishment after death; while the Pharisees who believed in reward and punishment at the end of days seem as yet to have had no clear notion of what was to happen to the soul in the interval.

In the course of the first century A.D. the Rabbis who carried on the work of Hillel and Shammai gradually discarded the use of the terms "end of days" and "Kingdom of Heaven" and substituted for them the term "future world" (Heb. *olam haba*, lit. "world that is to come"). Thus they no longer said of the Messiah that he would establish the Kingdom of Heaven, but that he would usher in the Future World, meaning apparently exactly the same thing.

They designated the places to which the souls of the righteous and the wicked respectively would be assigned in the future world as *Gan Eden* ("the Garden of Eden") and *Gehinnom* ("the Valley of Hinnom") respectively, and they seem even to have had some idea that this assignation might be made immediately after death.

By thus intercalating, as it were, the idea of the soul's survival into the Pharisaic eschatology, Hillel and Shammai and their successors gave a somewhat new colouring to Pharisaism, emphasizing its individualistic aspect. They contributed further to the same end by their activity in disseminating a knowledge of the Oral Law, and interest in it, much more widely than the Scribes had done, that is, beyond the circle of the Pharisees to the general public. They established the idea that the study of the Oral Law was equally meritorious with its performance (if, that is, it led to such performance), and created in the Jewish people a new intelligentsia known as *talmide chakhamim* (lit. "disciples of the wise," sing. *talmid chakham*), whose chief delight was to discuss questions of Jewish law both actual and hypothetical.

With the growth of this class the Pharisees as such lost their importance, and became merged in the general body of observant Jews. They could no longer vie with the Rabbis as the representatives of the Judaism of the Oral Law, and the proper title of that Judaism therefore, at least from the destruction of the Temple, if not from an earlier period, is no longer Pharisaism but Rabbinism.

CHAPTER III

RABBIS AND MINIM

WHILE the destruction of the Temple in A.D. 70 transformed Pharisaism into Rabbinism, it robbed Sadduceeism of its *raison d'être* by reducing priests to the level of laymen in the matter of religious service. No longer could the priesthood as such put forth any pretensions to the spiritual leadership of the Jewish people. In spite of this groups of Sadducees who clung to the ideas of the past in this matter, and hoped also for its restoration, continued to survive for centuries, but they soon sank into insignificance and played no further role in Jewish history, beyond keeping alive a spark which circumstances later fanned into a flame (*vide* Chapter iv). They no longer constituted a serious threat to Rabbinic Judaism, any more than the Samaritans. Not that the leadership of the Rabbis remained unchallenged; but the challenge came from a different quarter, and on quite a different issue.

In the latter period of the Second Temple, i.e., roughly the century before and the century after the beginning of the Christian era, the belief in the advent of a Messiah heralding the "end of days" was by no means confined to the Pharisees. We can see this clearly in the critical attitude towards Pharisaism of several of the apocalyptic writings in which that belief is proclaimed.

It is obvious from these that there were Jews in Palestine who, while sharing with the Pharisees the belief in the end of days and the kingdom of heaven, were by no means content with the Pharisaic way of preparing for it. Of one such sect, called Essenes or Essaioi, we have definite information. The members of this sect, we are told, in their preoccupation with the "affairs of heaven" went as far beyond the Pharisees as these beyond the Sadducees. They formed themselves into groups which led a monastic kind of existence, living with extreme frugality, devoting their time to prayer and contemplation, and taking no part or interest in the life around them. They seem too to have looked askance on the Temple service and probably had no high opinion of the intercession of the High Priest.

Like the Pharisees, the Essenes believed that the establishment of the kingdom of heaven would be preceded by the appearance of a heaven-sent deliverer whom they called the Messiah, or anointed. But they differed from them in their conception of this personage. The Pharisees attached to the name Messiah the same meaning as it has in the books of the Bible, namely, a duly anointed king of the House of David. As already mentioned, they believed that the establishment of the kingdom of heaven would be preceded, and perhaps ushered in, by the restoration of the kingdom of Israel under a monarch of the House of David, but they did not identify this restoration with the kingdom of heaven itself. The Essenes on the other hand seem to have ignored the restoration of the monarchy of Israel, and certainly conceived of the Messiah as the divinely appointed instrument for establishing the kingdom of God on earth.

In the early years of the Christian era there appeared in Judea a man named Johanan or John who proclaimed the near advent of the Messiah and called upon the people to prepare themselves for entering the kingdom of heaven. We do not know for certain whether he belonged to the Essenes, but he closely resembled them in his manner of life, especially in the great importance which he attached to ablutions in running water as a means of spiritual purification. He declared bathing in the Jordan to be the first step in moral regeneration, and for this reason was known as John the Baptist (i.e., bather).

Among those who came under the influence of John the Baptist was a young man from Nazareth in Galilee named Jesus (Hebrew "Yeshu," a shortened form of Joshua) son of Joseph. At some early period of his life Jesus conceived the idea that he was the heaven-sent Messiah whose coming had been announced by John the Baptist and whose mission it was to establish the kingdom of heaven on earth—whatever he may have meant by that expression.

Naturally the Sadducees, sceptical as they were about the kingdom of heaven in general, took no notice of his claim. Nor were the Pharisees, who looked upon the Essenes as mere visionaries, more likely to be favourably disposed towards him. He found a following, however, among the untutored working class, whose spiritual welfare was neglected by Sadducees and Pharisees alike. As might have been expected, his teaching brought him eventually into conflict with the Roman authorities, and he was executed by them before his movement obtained any wide extension.

The circumstances of Jesus's death made a deep impression on his followers and confirmed their belief in the divine character which they had already assigned to him in his lifetime. They were more convinced than ever that he was the Messiah. But since he had not in fact carried out the Messianic function of establishing the kingdom of God upon earth, they had to justify the title by linking it to some other aspect of his activity. This they found in the notion of an Intercessor, a being who would plead on their behalf with God and secure for them admission to the kingdom of heaven on the day of judgment. They regarded Jesus as a link between God and man, as the Son of God sent on earth to expiate the sins of men with his own blood, as the Redeemer through whose grace they would win eternal bliss.

At the same time they continued to observe the Mosaic law—more it would seem after the Essenic than the Pharisaic fashion. Thus, under the leadership of Jesus's chief disciple Peter they constituted a distinct sect, known in Hebrew as Nazarenes, apparently from Nazareth, the birthplace of Jesus, and in Greek as Christians, from *Christos*, the Greek for Messiah. Some, if not all of them, took vows of poverty and were therefore known as Ebionites (from the Hebrew *ebion*, poor), a name which their opponents mockingly applied to their alleged poverty of understanding.

Some thirty years after the death of Jesus a Pharisee named Saul of Tarsus, having become converted to a belief in the divinity of Jesus, proclaimed that those who relied upon his intercession had no need of the Mosaic law, and so transformed Judeo-Christianity into Christianity pure and simple.

The Pharisees of Jerusalem and Palestine were no more inclined to listen to Paul than they had been to listen to Jesus thirty years before. So long as the Temple existed they clung tenaciously to their belief in the efficacy of the priestly service, even though since the time of Herod many of the High Priests had been notoriously corrupt. But when the Temple was destroyed in A.D. 70 they were compelled to revise their position.

For a time, it is true, they could take refuge in the hope that the Temple would be soon rebuilt, that the interruption of the priestly service would prove to be only temporary, as it had been two or three centuries before, when the Temple was desecrated by the Syrian king Antiochus. This hope, however, faded away when the attempt of Bar Cochba to recover Jerusalem from the Romans ended in disaster in 135; and the Rabbinic Jews were forced to take seriously the challenge of the Judeo-Christians.

The principal response of the Rabbis to this challenge was to emphasize to a much greater extent than the Pharisees had done the value of the *mitzvah*, the performance of the religious precept, for the salvation of the individual soul. They inculcated the idea that the individual, for the salvation of his soul, could rely entirely upon his own efforts, and did not need even the mediation of a High Priest. The performance of any *mitzvah* was in itself a passport to *olam haba*, the future world. The Pharisees had observed the *mitzvoth* primarily as a means of uniting them organically with the people of Israel as a whole. It was the people which obtained merit in the sight of God through the Temple service and the mediation of the High Priest, and the individual participated in that merit through carrying out the commandments. But the Rabbis now taught that the performance of the precepts was a direct source of merit to the individual independently of the people. Thus it became possible to dispense with the Temple service as a source of salvation.

This idea is succinctly expressed in a dictum of Rabbi Eleazar ben Jacob, an authority of the latter part of the second century: "He who performs one precept acquires for himself one advocate (in the final judgment), and he who commits one transgression acquires for himself one accuser."[1] The assertion that the performance of the precept itself pleads, as it were, on behalf of the doer seems to be meant as a denial of the Christian view that the intercession of Jesus was necessary for salvation. A further indication of this is provided by the fact that the word used for "advocate" in this dictum is *praklit*, the Hebraised form of the Greek word *paracletos*, in place of the more usual *s'negor*, the Hebraised form of the Greek *synegoros* (and in fact the word used for accuser in this passage is the corresponding *kategor*, the Hebraised form of *kategoros*).

We know that Jesus was commonly called by the Christians "the Paraclete." It would seem therefore that the Rabbi deliberately meant to suggest to the Jews that their Paraclete was the *mitzvah* and not Jesus. A similar suggestion seems to be contained in another Rabbinical dictum of the same period: "God desired to make Israel worthy (of salvation), therefore he gave them a great quantity of law and precepts"—a plain hint that the way to salvation for the Jew lay not in reliance on Jesus but in the performance of the precepts.

Equally it was part of the Rabbinical teaching that the Jewish people had not forfeited its hope of a national redemption through its rejection of Jesus. As the seed of Abraham, Isaac and Jacob it could rely on *zekhuth aboth*, "the merit of the patriarchs," for procuring this boon, even independently of their own merit, though this could hasten it. "If all Israel," said one authority, "were to keep properly two consecutive Sabbaths, they would be at once redeemed," while another found a similar idea in the words of the prophet (Isaiah lx, 22), "I the Lord will hasten it in its time," which he paraphrased: "If Israel is worthy, I will hasten it (the redemption); if not, it will come in its due time."

The fact that the Jew was now precluded from carrying out those precepts which depended on the existence of the Temple, and that those who lived outside of Palestine—as most even of the Rabbis themselves soon came to do—were

[1] *Aboth* iv.

precluded from carrying out many precepts which were bound up with the soil of that country, made no difference to the Rabbinic belief in the *torah* as the sole means of Israel's salvation both individually and nationally. There were still enough *mitzvoth* left to procure for the observant Jew his share in the future world, and on these the Rabbis now concentrated their attention, elaborating them in even greater detail than the Scribes and earlier Rabbis had done.

They subjected the Mishnah (*vide* p. 35) to a minute analysis, for the purpose of discovering the principles which underlay its decision, and so enabling themselves to deal with the new problems of Jewish law to which the altered circumstances of the people were giving rise. This process was carried out concurrently and independently by the Rabbis in Palestine and in Babylonia, where the Jewish community under the Arsacid Parthian dynasty had awakened to new life at the beginning of the third century. In Palestine the process went on for some two centuries, i.e., till about the end of the fourth century, in Babylon for about a hundred years longer. The analysis of the Mishnah was carried on mostly in the Aramaic language—now the chief vernacular of the Jews—and was called by the Hebrew name *talmud* (study), or more frequently by the Aramaic equivalent *gemara*. The *gemara* of the leading authorities was interwoven with the Mishnah in the form of a running commentary, and like the Mishnah was always memorized and transmitted orally. While, however, there was only one Mishnah, there were two Gemaras, a Palestinian and a Babylonian, the latter of which considerably excelled the former in legal acumen and comprehensiveness. When each Gemara was completed, it formed with the Mishnah a single book, called in the one case the Palestinian and in the other the Babylonian Talmud; and these—especially the latter—became rather than the Mishnah by itself the authoritative embodiment of Jewish law.

Actually there was something more in each Talmud than the law. In each of them were inserted large numbers of *obiter dicta* of the Rabbis on a great variety of subjects— interpretations of biblical texts, moral aphorisms, legendary and biographical anecdotes, and many other matters. The whole of this material was known by the name of *haggadah* (lit. "telling"). Though differing widely in character from the *halakhah*, it was regarded as being equally an integral part of the Talmud, and though of lighter texture was treated with hardly less respect. Thus as the Talmud in its totality consisted of two parts, the Mishnah and the Gemara, so the Gemara also consisted of two parts, the *halakhah* and the *haggadah*, the latter being interwoven into the former in a rather haphazard fashion.

The Rabbis called the Judeo-Christians *Minim*, a word of uncertain origin which seems to mean "sectaries." Certainly it was applied by the Rabbis not only to the Judeo-Christians (and to Christian controversialists), but to all Jewish sectaries who tampered with the monotheistic belief of Judaism. Chief among these in the second and third centuries were the Jewish Gnostics, who maintained that there were two Powers, one of good and one of evil. The Gnostics had really very little in common with the Judeo-Christians, and many of them were bitter enemies of Christianity. The Rabbis, however, classed them together because in both they saw a danger to the monotheistic creed.

The Jewish Gnostics were led to their belief in two Powers primarily, no doubt, by a desire to explain the existence of evil in the world, and especially the sufferings of the Jewish people. But ostensibly they based this belief on their interpretation of the Scriptures, especially of the first two or three chapters of Genesis, and in particular of the text "And God said, Let *us* make man in *our* image, after *our* likeness" (Gen. i, 26). The attitude of the Rabbis to these Gnostics is well illustrated by a statement reported by R. Samuel bar Nachman in the name of R. Jonathan—both Palestinian authorities of the third century: "When Moses was transcribing the *torah* (from God's dictation), he wrote the account of each day (of the creation). When he came to the verse 'Let us make man, etc.,' he said before the Almighty: 'Sovereign of the Universe, why dost Thou give an opening to the *minim*?' God replied: 'Do thou write, and he who wishes to err, let him err'." Undoubtedly those who "wished to err" in this way constituted a serious threat to Rabbinic Judaism.

As the Gnostics sought to prove from the Bible the plurality of Gods, so the Judeo-Christians and Christians sought to prove the Messiahship of Jesus. The Rabbis naturally could not pay less attention to their own Scriptures than their enemies; and accordingly the homiletic exposition of the Scriptures became an essential part of their activity, in addition to the teaching of the *halakhah*; some of them in fact specialized on this branch.

This exposition was called by the name *midrash* or inquiry, the same name as was applied to the legal glosses of the ancient Scribes (*vide supra*, p. 33). Some of these expositions—those which were thought to bear a particularly *ex cathedra* character—were included in the *haggadah* of the Talmud (*vide supra*, p. 44). Many of the rest were carefully preserved, and in later times (from the fifth to the tenth century) were formed into compilations which bore the general title of *midrashim* and were reduced to writing.

The *haggadah* and the *midrash* enormously strengthened the hold of the Rabbis on the Jewish public. They possessed a popular appeal which was lacking in the stern and forbidding *halakhah*, and thus enabled the Rabbis to add persuasion to authority in inculcating the Jewish religion. Nor did the Rabbis omit to furnish the masses with a defence against *minuth*—as the doctrines of the *minim* were called—which was independent of their own teaching. This was the formulation of a liturgy both for public and for private prayer, which they declared to possess the same efficacy for religious purposes as the sacrifices of old.

The central feature of this liturgy was the recital morning and evening of the verse Deuteronomy vi, 4: "Hear, O Israel, the Lord our God, the Lord is one." This practice dated back to early times, but it was given a new significance by the Rabbis by being brought into connection with the following gloss on the first of the Ten Commandments ("I am the Lord thy God who brought thee out of the land of Egypt"): "God said to the Israelites, Accept My sovereignty and thereafter ye shall receive My commandments." The recital of the words "Hear, O Israel, etc."—the precise meaning of which is a matter of debate—was declared to be the proper manner of "accepting the yoke of the kingdom of heaven," and so creating the proper frame of mind for the performance of the precepts. This formula therefore, known in Hebrew as the *shma'* from its opening word, became the Jew's standard confession of faith, and it has remained such for practically all sections of Jews up to the present day.

CHAPTER IV

RABBANITES AND KARAITES

AT the time when the compilation of the Babylonian Talmud was completed, towards the end of the fifth century (*vide supra*, p. 43), the Jewish people exhibited an unusual degree of uniformity in religious practice and outlook. This was due to the immense prestige and authority enjoyed by the so-called "Gaonim,"[1] the heads of the two great Talmudical academies at Pumbeditha and Sura in Babylonia. From these academies went out teachers and spiritual guides to Jewish communities throughout the world, and to them were addressed questions on Jewish law from all parts.

The Samaritans, it is true, were still strong in Palestine, and there were still perhaps isolated communities of Sadducees and even of Judeo-Christians. But for the greater part of the Jewish people Judaism meant Rabbinic or Talmudic Judaism, and of this Judaism the Gaonim were the authoritative exponents.

The first recorded challenge to the authority of the Gaonim came about the middle of the eighth century from a man named Abu Isa of Isfahan, who proclaimed himself to be a Messiah and is said to have gathered round himself a following of ten thousand men. In his capacity of Messiah Abu Isa took the liberty of interpreting certain precepts of the *torah* in his own way. He did not, however, contest the authority of the Gaonim in general and he created no schism. In any case his attempt to redeem the Jews failed and his following was soon dissolved.

A much more serious rival to the Gaonim was Anan son of David, who appeared on the scene soon after Abu Isa. According to an account which became current in later days,

[1] The word *gaon* in Hebrew signifies "excellency," but the title seems to have been Persian in origin.

47

Anan in 760 became a candidate for the post of *Resh Galutha* or Exilarch, the supreme secular authority among the Jews of Babylonia, and a dignitary of considerable power and influence in the kingdom of the Caliph. The Gaonim, in whose hands the appointment lay, passed him over in favour of his younger brother, and their action was confirmed by the Caliph. Anan thereupon declared himself Exilarch and gathered round himself a considerable following. He was in consequence brought to trial in Bagdad for rebelling against the Caliph, and saved himself only by declaring that he did not accept the authority of the Gaonim in religious matters.

The whole story is of somewhat doubtful authenticity, especially the last-named incident. What is certain, however, is that Anan, who was well versed in the Talmud, set himself to work out a new form of Judaism which should be independent of Rabbinic authority. Whether he had any other motive besides his jealousy of the Gaonim and perhaps a desire to show off his own cleverness we cannot say.[1]

The fruit of his labours was seen in a book which he published about 770, under the title of *Sefer ha-Mitzvoth*, "Book of the Precepts." This book, written in Aramaic, is very similar in style to the *midrash* of the Scribes and their followers on th eprecepts of the Pentateuch (*vide supra*, p. 34). It interprets the text by means of the same hermeneutical rules as those employed by the Rabbis. But it applies them in a highly reckless and arbitrary fashion, and in many cases comes to conclusions quite different from those of the Rabbis. Thus it produced an *halakhah* or Jewish way of life differing widely from that prescribed in the Mishnah and Talmud.

Unlike the Rabbis, who followed established custom wherever possible, Anan professed to derive the whole of his regulations from the text of the Scriptures. Actually he seems to have borrowed from various sources—from the Mishnah itself on the one hand, and from the Sadducees and Abu Isa on the other. But in all cases he made a point of finding a warrant for his conclusions somewhere or other in the *mikra* or

---

[1] It is possible that Anan was influenced consciously or unconsciously by the example of the Mohammedan sect of Shiites who in his day rejected the Islamic tradition and accepted the authority of the Koran only.

Scriptures. In this way he sought to render the Talmud superfluous for the determining of Jewish law. On the other hand, he claimed no infallibility for his own interpretations of the Scripture, and so left the field open for the exercise of individual judgment.

It was perhaps this feature in Anan's teaching which appealed most strongly to his contemporaries. Certainly he did not aim at making Judaism any easier for them. It became in his hands a more austere and burdensome form of religion than that of the Rabbis. The Mishnah, although it multiplied immensely the number of precepts to be carried out, yet in many cases mitigated the severity of the original Scriptural rule. The Rabbis always bore in mind the principle that "no burden is to be laid on the public which it is unable to bear."

Anan had much less consideration for the weakness of human nature. He seemed in fact to go out of his way to make the religion harder. Thus in its interpretation of the precept "Ye shall kindle no fire in all your dwellings on the Sabbath day" (Exod. xxxv, 3), the Mishnah was content with the plain meaning of the words, and allowed a fire or light which had been kindled before Sabbath to be left burning throughout the Sabbath. Anan, however, by a piece of extraordinary casuistry, deduced the rule that on the approach of the Sabbath all fires and lights which were still burning had to be extinguished.

Another factor which brought Anan adherents may have been the idea that by rejecting the authority of the Gaonim they would ingratiate themselves with the Mohammedan authorities. It is this idea which was attributed to Anan in the story mentioned above, and it may well have affected consciously or unconsciously many of his contemporaries. For whatever reason large numbers of Jews soon accepted Anan as their teacher, adopting his methods of interpreting the Scripture and following more or less the way of life prescribed in his Book of Precepts.

From their devotion to the *mikra* (Scripture, *vide* p. 19) the Ananites were by the other Jews called also *Ba'ale Mikra* ("students of the *mikra*") or *Karaim* ("Readers," sing. *kara*). The title *kara* had formerly been borne by those scholars who preserved the correct tradition of the reading of the Hebrew

Scriptures in the days when they were still written without vowel-points, i.e., up to some time in the eighth century. Whether the Ananites derived any of their interpretations from the ancient *karaim* we do not know, but it seems not unlikely. The Karaites on their side gave the name of Rabbanites to those Jews who still accepted the authority of the Gaonim.

The liberty exercised by the individual Karaites in the interpretation of the Scriptures led to a great diversity of practice among them. Anan's "Book of the Precepts" soon became antiquated, but for some time there was no other code to take its place. A considerable measure of uniformity was introduced among them by Benjamin of Nahawend, in Persia, who flourished in the middle of the ninth century, and enjoyed an authority among the Karaites scarcely second to that of Anan himself.

Benjamin was an Arabic scholar, and he applied Arabic philological science to the study of the Hebrew Scriptures; hence his interpretations carried weight. He showed himself much less hostile to the Rabbinic tradition than Anan had been, and adopted many rules from the Mishnah. Nevertheless he rather accentuated than mitigated the character of austerity which had been imprinted on Karaism by its founder. Thus whereas Anan, agreeing for once with the Rabbis, had declared the laws of Levitical purity to be abrogated with the destruction of the Temple, Benjamin Nahawendi pronounced them to be still obligatory. Some branches of the Karaites went even further in the same direction and became pronounced ascetics.

Unlike Anan, Benjamin Nahawendi did not confine his lucubrations to the precepts but he explored also the field of dogma and belief. The Rabbis had already insisted on the complete incorporeality of God, and the anthropomorphic expressions applied to God in the Pentateuch were carefully paraphrased in the *targum*, the authorized Aramaic translation of it in use among the Jews since the first century. Under the influence of the Mohammedan school of theologians called Mutazilites, Benjamin went much further and declared that all interventions of God upon earth, such as the appearance on Mount Sinai, were performed through an intermediary. In this doctrine, however, only a small section of the Karaites, known as Makarites or Magharites, seems to have followed him.

In spite of its austerity—perhaps even because of it, for the ninth century was a period of religious fervour—Karaism exercised a powerful attractive force on the Jews in Babylonia and Palestine and spread rapidly, reaching even as far afield as Spain. It naturally drew to itself those who for whatever reason chafed at the domination of the Gaonim. It also appealed strongly to the growing number of Jews who were adopting Arabic instead of Aramaic as their ordinary language. Difference of language created a gulf between such Jews and the teachers of the Talmud, who still used exclusively Aramaic, and made them impervious to their influence.

On the other hand, in the Karaites, who largely used Arabic, they found teachers whom they could understand. No wonder therefore that at the end of the ninth century Karaism was threatening to displace Rabbanism as the dominant form of the Jewish religion throughout the East.

From this fate Judaism was saved principally by the efforts of one man, Saadiah ben Joseph, who at the critical moment came forward as a champion of Rabbinism. Saadiah was born at Fayyoum in Upper Egypt in 892 (or according to some 882), and in his early years managed in some way to acquire both a Talmudic and an Arabic education, becoming highly proficient in both branches. Unlike most of the Arabic-trained youth of the time, however, he remained a staunch adherent of Rabbanism.

At an early age he threw himself into the controversy which had long been raging between the Karaites and the Rabbanites, with a work in Arabic called *The Refutation of Anan* in which he exposed the self-contradictions in the Karaite position, showing that without the aid of the oral tradition preserved in the Mishnah and Talmud it was impossible to carry out the Mosaic religion. He followed this up with a number of other polemical works—some in Hebrew and some in Arabic—to which the Karaites were unable to find any satisfactory reply, and which therefore effectively stayed the advance of Karaism.

Saadiah—who in 928 became the Gaon of the Academy of Sura—was able to refute the Karaites because he had himself absorbed all that was valuable in Karaism. Like them he was a close student of the Scripture, and like them too he applied to the elucidation of the text a knowledge of Hebrew grammar and philology which was sadly lacking in his fellow Rabbanites. But he applied this knowledge in a way of his own, which was very different from theirs. He did not attempt by means of it to controvert either the jurisprudence or the ethic of the Rabbis. He accepted without demur their teaching in these fields, based as it was on the Talmud and the Midrash. He used his superior understanding of the Scripture for a different and highly novel purpose, namely, to lay the foundations of a Jewish culture which should weave into the teaching of the *torah* the most precious results of Arabic thought and inquiry.

The principal work by means of which Saadiah brought about this innovation was his Arabic translation of, and commentary on, the Hebrew Scriptures (completed about 930). Hitherto systematic commentaries on biblical books had been composed only by Karaites, but Saadiah now showed himself incomparably superior to all of them as an exegete. Like them he made it his chief effort to discover the literal meaning of the text, but unlike them he did not strain the meaning in order to extract from it some rule of conduct.

Apart from this, he introduced in his commentary considerable quantities of Arabic learning, often without any great relevance to the text in hand. In the eyes of the modern student this is a blemish, but to his fellow Rabbanites, who interpreted the Scripture chiefly through the medium of the homiletic midrash, these digressions came as a revelation both of the literary beauties of the Bible and of the wealth of Arabic culture. They opened out to the Talmudical students new vistas which they could not forbear to explore. Henceforth the methodical study of the Bible, and with it of the Hebrew language, became an integral part of the Rabbinic curriculum and a knowledge of Arabic culture became a desideratum for every Jewish student.

Thus through its conflict with Karaism Rabbinic Judaism acquired a richer content, a brighter hue, as it were. It became a culture as well as a religion properly so called. It was a religion in virtue of making the "saving of souls" and the "future world" its chief objective. But it became a culture through recognizing that the cultivation of the mind was also a desirable object, even from a religious point of view, provided it was carried out in such a way as to impart a deeper understanding and a heightened appreciation of the Hebrew Scriptures. Naturally it was not always easy to draw the line between cultivation of the mind as an adjunct to religion and cultivating it for its own sake—between the Hebraic and the Hellenic objectives.

In theory the Jewish scholars of the Arabic period always followed the former course; their most secular studies were supposed to be *ad majorem Dei laudem*, and were intended to assist their understanding of the Scriptures or of the nature of God. Whether in practice they were always able to observe the distinction is not so certain.

None the less it may be said that for some three centuries after Saadiah the Arabic-speaking Jews combined in a harmonious culture the study first of the Hebrew Scriptures, secondly of the Talmud and Rabbinic literature, and thirdly of Arabic literature, to which they themselves made notable contributions. During this period they produced a rich and varied literature, partly in Hebrew, partly in Arabic, which expressed Jewish thought in Arabic literary forms.

At the end of the tenth century Spain became the great centre of Jewish culture, and it remained such after the Arabs were displaced over the greater part of the country by the Christians, in the thirteenth century. Under Christian rule the Jews ultimately forgot Arabic, but the Saadian impulse still continued to act upon them, though with diminished power, and Hebrew works infused with his spirit of rational inquiry combined with reverence for authority continued to be produced up to the expulsion of the Jews from Spain in 1492.

The culture of the Arabic-speaking Jews blossomed forth in various branches of literary production, parallel with those of Arabic literature. The following may be specified as having issued directly from the study of the Scriptures, and as having contributed in no small degree to fix the form of the Jewish religion both in belief and in practice.

(1) The first of these branches was the methodical exegesis

of the Bible in the Hebrew language, known in Hebrew as *perush* (explanation). This exegesis differed from that of the midrash in being essentially philological in character, not homiletical; its first object was to set forth what the Bible said, not what it taught. Its cultural value lay primarily in the fact that it exhibited the Bible as a Hebrew book or collection of books, and not merely as a collection of texts. By so doing it kept alive in the Jewish people the interest in the Hebrew language, and stimulated the desire to use it for literary purposes, itself setting the example.

As the fountain-head of the Hebrew language the Bible acquired in the eyes of the Jews a new value which strengthened its religious hold on them. The first notable representative of this style of exegesis was the French Jew Solomon ben Isaac (1030–1100), commonly known as Rashi, who, however, is still partly midrashic or homiletical. More typical was the Spanish scholar Abraham ibn Ezra (1092–1167), who in his literary approach to the Bible carried on the tradition of Saadiah. It was from Rashi and Ibn Ezra and other medieval commentators who followed in their wake that the Jews for many centuries derived their understanding of the Bible.

(2) A second branch in which Judeo-Arabic culture manifested itself was the composition of devotional poetry in Hebrew, on the model of the Psalms. Three writers, all from Spain, particularly distinguished themselves in this field— Solomon ibn-Gabirol (fl. *c.* 1050), Moses ibn-Ezra (1070– *c.* 1140), and Jehudah ha-Levi (*c.* 1085–*c.* 1140). Although they derived their inspiration from the Psalms, these writers were not mere imitators of the Scriptural poetry. They used Arabic metres, and gave poetic expression to their own religious and spiritual experience. The Hebrew which they wrote was purely biblical, but they imparted to it an extraordinary variety, flexibility and melodiousness. They wrote primarily for the individual seeking communion with God. Several of their poems, however, have been deemed suitable for public worship, and have been embodied in the synagogue liturgy.

(3) From the Arabs the Jews learnt to reflect upon their religious faith and to reduce it to definite dogmas. Through the medium of Arabic translations they obtained access to the

works of the Neo-Platonists and also of Aristotle and Plato. Here they found set forth certain fundamental principles which commended themselves to their reason, and they had to decide whether acceptance of them would in any way conflict with their religion. For this purpose they were under the necessity of defining their faith and making clear to themselves what it was that they really believed, and also why. This task was first attempted by Saadiah in a book written towards the end of his life in Arabic, under the title of *El-I'tikadat w'al-Amanat* (Beliefs and Opinions). In the course of the next three centuries a number of other works were written with the same object, of which the most famous was the *Guide to the Perplexed* of Moses ben Maimun, or Maimonides (1135-1204). Though originally written in Arabic, these works were all translated into Hebrew, and became integral parts of the new Hebraic culture.

Besides this elaborate work on the Jewish faith, Maimonides also in another of his works took occasion to formulate his faith in thirteen short statements each commencing with the words, "I believe with a perfect faith." These creeds, as they were called, are open to various strictures if presented as a complete expression of Jewish faith. Nevertheless they were a close enough approximation to satisfy a need which was strongly felt by the mass of the people. They were therefore generally adopted as the standard definition of the Jewish faith, and were given a place in the prayer book.

(4) Another task which Maimonides set himself was to codify the whole of Jewish law, which now embraced a vast multitude of regulations. For this purpose he wrote his great Hebrew work called *Mishneh Torah* (lit. "repetition of the law"). His avowed object was merely to enable the student to find the law on any subject without having to search for it through the whole of the Talmud and the later decisions.

In fact, however, he achieved much more than this. He correlated the Talmudic law, on the one hand with the ethical principles underlying it, on the other hand with the law of the Pentateuch. He thus gave it a certain philosophical flavour, besides bringing it closer in spirit to the Bible, the influence of which is also clearly apparent in his elegant Hebrew style. Hence his work had a high cultural as well as legal value.

Maimonides's code did not prove so serviceable as he had expected, because in some respects it was too comprehensive, including for instance the laws of the sacrifices, which were now only of academic interest, while it was not detailed enough in some matters affecting the daily life of the Jew. Subsequent scholars, therefore, basing themselves on his work, composed codes of more immediate practical utility, incidentally correcting a number of legal errors which he had made.

The last of these codes, called *Shulchan Arukh* (lit. "laid table"), was composed by Joseph Caro, a Jew of Spanish origin who lived at Safed in Palestine in the middle of the sixteenth century. This code was severely practical; while eschewing all superfluous matter, including reasons and references, it aimed at regulating the life of the conforming Jew down to the smallest details. It was accepted by Jews all over the world as authoritative, and became along with the thirteen creeds of Maimonides the standard of Jewish orthodoxy. None the less it did not displace the *Mishneh Torah*, which remained the great textbook for the principles of Jewish law. Thus Maimonides became in a sense the law-giver of subsequent generations, a fact to which his admirers gave expression in the well-known saying, "From Moses to Moses there arose not like Moses."

In the production of this Hebraic culture the Karaites took practically no part, though they had given the first impulse to it. The reason no doubt was that they lacked the intellectual stimulus which the Rabbanites derived from the study of the Talmud—both from the casuistry and dialectic of the *halakhah* and from the imagery of the *haggadah*. They never again rose to the literary height which had been reached by their biblical commentators in the ninth and tenth centuries. Only one work produced by them after this period became known to the outside world. This was a polemic against Christianity called *Chizzuk Emunah* (Strengthening of Faith) written in 1594 by Isaac Troki, of Troki in Lithuania. It was translated into several languages and was declared by Voltaire to be the most complete refutation of Christian doctrine which he had ever seen.

When Spain became the chief centre of Jewish settlement in the eleventh century, Karaism found only an insecure footing there, but it continued to flourish for some time in the East.

When, however, Maimonides settled in Cairo at the end of the twelfth century, his fame so impressed the Karaites that many of them came over to Rabbanism, and from that time the movement began to decline. Towards the end of the Middle Ages Karaite settlements were formed in the Crimea and in Lithuania, and these survived the disappearance of Karaism in Asia.

When the Russian Government began to persecute the Jews in the nineteenth century, it spared the Karaites on the ground that they rejected the Talmud. To make their position still more secure, the Karaites of the Crimea persuaded the Russian authorities by means of forged documents that they had been settled there since before the Christian era, and therefore bore no part in the responsibility for the crucifixion. Their numbers, however, continued to dwindle, and at the end of the nineteenth century it was computed that there were not more than about 10,000 of them in the Crimea and 2,000 in Lithuania.[1]

[1] The former group has suffered severely from the anti-religious policy of the Soviet Government and also from the ravages of the Second World War, in consequence of which the latter group was entirely uprooted. The only Karaite body of any importance which still survives is the thriving but intellectually stagnant community in Cairo and its neighbourhood.

CHAPTER V

MAIMUNISTS AND ANTI-MAIMUNISTS

To Jewish as to Mohammedan students, the study of Greek philosophy to which they began to apply themselves from about the beginning of the ninth century provided at once a precious stimulus to thought and a challenge to their religious belief. Here subjects on which their own sacred books laid down the law dogmatically were treated in a spirit of free inquiry and rational investigation. That this was a right and proper way of treating them seemed self-evident to all who possessed a philosophic bent of mind. Free inquiry was the note of Arabic culture; and these books showed them how to carry it into the field of religious belief as well. On the other hand, Greek philosophy was a dangerous edge tool, as it frequently arrived at results greatly at variance with the teaching of revealed religion.

As might have been expected, the study of philosophy showed itself from an early period to be inimical to religious orthodoxy. It bred scepticism with regard to religious belief and indifference to religious practice. An Arabic poet complained at the end of the ninth century that "while some have insight but no faith, others have faith but no understanding." A notable instance of such irreligion was presented by a Jew named Chivi of Balch in Bactria who at the end of the ninth century wrote a scathing attack on the Bible, charging it with all kinds of contradictions and absurdities.

To counteract the noxious effects of the study of philosophy while retaining its benefits, the Mohammedan theologians developed a kind of religious philosophy, called the *kalam*, which among other things aimed at interpreting the text of the Koran in such a way as to make it consonant with Greek philosophical requirements. Saadiah attempted a similar task for the Jews in parts of his commentary on the Bible, (*vide* p. 52). He carried this attempt further in his book *Beliefs and Opinions* (*v. supra* p. 55), written towards the end of his life, in which he set forth systematically the fundamental tenets of the Jewish religion and tried to show that in no point did they contradict the dictates of reason. This work was widely read among the Jews and helped many generations to combine the study of the Bible and Talmud with that of philosophy.

For Saadiah philosophy meant certain works of the Neo-Platonist school which were all that had been translated, or at any rate all that were usually studied, in his day. As other and more profound works obtained the ascendancy in the Arabic philosophical schools, it became necessary to tackle afresh and from somewhat different angles the problem of reconciling Judaism with philosophy. The chief works in which this task was attempted were the *Duties of the Heart*, of Bachya ibn Pakuda, written about 1060, the *Chozari* of Jehudah ha-Levi (*c.* 1140), the *Lofty Faith* of Abraham ibn Daud (*c.* 1170), and finally the *Guide to the Perplexed* of Moses Maimonides (1190). This by its comprehensiveness and profundity threw all the others in the shade, and was read with avidity by Jewish students.

It is worthy of note that all these works of Jewish religious philosophy were written in Arabic and not in Hebrew. One reason for this was probably that the authors considered them to be of more than purely Jewish interest, being as they were in some parts a defence of revealed religion in general against the arguments of rationalism, and they therefore addressed themselves to the educated Arabic world at large. Another reason may well have been that they did not wish to press their views on those of their fellow-Jews whose intellectual interest lay mainly in the study of the Talmud, and who looked on philosophy with some mistrust.

Actually there was little if anything in the Pre-Maimunist works which could have given offence to such people. If the authors did not defend everything in the Jewish religion, they nowhere implied that there was anything in it indefensible. If they sought to show that revealed religion was in harmony with reason, they nowhere hinted that reason in itself possessed an authority superior to that of revelation. Maimonides, however, was not so restrained. Steeped as he was in the teaching of Aristotle, he asserted openly that in a conflict between reason and authority the last word should lie with reason; and he was not afraid to draw from this principle certain conclusions which he knew would shock some of his co-religionists.[1]

Not that Maimonides was in any sense what we should call today a free-thinker. He knew how to define authority and reason in such a way as to leave the prerogative of the Bible at any rate unaffected. He made no effort to gloss over the fact that the teaching of the Bible conflicted in some fundamental points with that of Aristotle. He denied, however, that the former was to be rejected on this account. For, on the one hand, even Aristotle was after all not the last word of reason, and on some points—notably the doctrine of *creatio ex nihilo*—it was permissible to differ from him on purely rational grounds. And on the other hand the Hebrew Scriptures in critical passages admitted of a variety of interpretations, and it would always be possible to find among them one which would be consonant with any conclusion definitely established by reason.

With the Talmud Maimonides dealt rather more cavalierly. While acknowledging the binding character of the Oral Law or *halakhah* in general, he insisted on the need for seeking out the reasons of the various precepts of the Pentateuch in order to decide on the exact way in which they were to be performed. As for the haggadic part of the Talmud, he denied to it any authority whatever, and had no scruple in rejecting, as contrary to reason, certain ideas and beliefs derived from the *haggadah* which had become firmly implanted in Rabbinic Judaism.

Chief among these was the resuscitation of the body at the final judgment. Maimonides also propounded a rationalistic theory of prophecy, as a purely psychological phenomenon, which was widely different from the picture painted by the *haggadah*; and while he sought carefully to explain away the anthropomorphic and anthropopathic expressions applied to

[1] See Leon Roth's volume in this series, *The Guide for the Perplexed: Moses Maimonides*.

the Deity in the Bible, those which occurred in the *haggadah* he simply dismissed as mere flights of imagination.

Being written in Arabic, Maimonides's *Guide* circulated at first only in Mohammedan countries, and chiefly in Spain, where Arabic culture was most widely diffused among the Jews. Here his views on the relation of authority and reason were on the whole accepted by the educated classes; at any rate they were not actively opposed. Not that there were wanting scholars to whom they were utterly repugnant.

Conspicuous among these was Meir Abulafia (1180-1244), a learned Talmudist from Toledo. When Maimonides had first published in an earlier work his views on the resurrection and the nature of immortality, Abulafia had taken violent exception to them, and had sent a circular letter to "the wise men of Lunel" in Provence denouncing them. He had, however, found no support—on the contrary, he had been sharply censured by some of those whom he approached—and though he bitterly resented Maimonides's attitude to the Talmud, he now judged it better to hold his peace.

In the field of religious practice the study of the *Guide* produced effects similar to those produced by the study of philosophy in general in earlier days. Many found in it grounds for religious laxity and for a disbelief in the Bible and Talmud. Some were so corrupted by it as to marry out of their faith. Nor were these effects confined to Spain. In 1204 the *Guide* was translated into Hebrew by a Provençal Jew named Samuel ibn Tibbon—whose father, Judah ibn Tibbon, had already translated the other principal Jewish works of the same stamp—and so made accessible to the Jews of Provence, whose intellectual interests were similar to those of the Spanish Jews; and before long the corruption spread in Provence also.

In the opinion of Talmudists of the stamp of Abulafia—of whom there were many in Provence and not a few in Spain—the best if not the only way to stop this corruption was by restoring the authority of the Talmud against the encroachments of reason. A determined effort to do so was made by Solomon ben Abraham, a Rabbi of Montpellier in 1232, some twenty-eight years after Maimonides's death. Filled as he was with reverence for the Talmud, Solomon was deeply shocked by many of the ideas of Maimonides, and was anxious above all things to prevent them from spreading. In view of the enormous prestige enjoyed by Maimonides he could see no other way of accomplishing this than by preventing his heretical works from being read altogether. To secure this end he determined to follow the example set by the Church in similar circumstances and place them under a ban.

Such a ban to be effective required according to Jewish custom the signature of at least three Rabbis; and its weight was strictly proportionate to the moral authority enjoyed by its signatories. Solomon found it no easy matter to obtain fellow signatories of sufficient weight. Not a single Rabbi in Provence would join with him; but at length two of his former disciples consented to support him, Jonah ben Abraham, a highly esteemed Rabbi of Gerona in Spain, and David ben Saul.

Early in 1232 these three pronounced a sentence of excommunication against all who should read the philosophical works of Maimonides—that is, the *Guide* and the first section of his legal codex, the *Mishneh Torah*, against all who should occupy themselves with any subject of study outside of the Bible and Talmud, against all who should seek to explain away the literal meaning of the Bible, and all who should explain the *haggadah* differently from the great popular exegete Rashi. In a statement giving their reasons for this step which they issued at the same time, they emphasized their belief that the ideas of Maimonides with regard to the Talmud were undermining Judaism. They even cast doubts on his own personal orthodoxy, at any rate in his later years.

The ban caused a schism in Provence and Spain such as Jewry had not known for many years. Everywhere communities were divided into Maimunists and anti-Maimunists. In the three chief communities of Provence—Lunel, Bezières and Narbonne—the former were in the ascendant, and they replied to Solomon's ban with one on himself and his colleagues. In Montpellier opinion was divided, and the opposing parties more than once came to blows. Controversy raged bitterly throughout Catalonia, Aragon and Castile. David Kimchi, the famous biblical commentator of Narbonne, now in his seventy-third year, declared himself in favour of Maimonides.

On the other hand, Nachmanides (Moses ben Nachman, 1194-1270), the leading Talmudical scholar of Spain, sided with Solomon, as also naturally did Meir Abulafia in Toledo. The Rabbis of North France also supported the ban, though there was little danger at that time that the study of philosophy would spread to their region; and in fact on this ground many of them soon withdrew their support.

In a letter addressed to the communities of Aragon in August 1232, Bachiel Alconstantin and other supporters of Maimonides carried the war into the enemy's camp, asserting that the opponents of secular learning were in conflict with the Talmud itself. "Our Sages," they said, "inculcate the duty of conceiving the unity of God philosophically. We have to know profane sciences in order to be able to answer the opponents of religion. Astronomy, geometry, and other branches which are necessary for religion itself we cannot learn from the Talmud. ... It is a religious duty to acquire general knowledge." In consequence of this letter the chief communities of Aragon imposed the ban on Solomon and his coadjutors.

A little later the aged David Kimchi summoned Jehudah Alfachar, the most influential Jew in Toledo, which was the chief Jewish community in Spain, to declare himself in favour of Maimonides and so bring the conflict to an end. Alfachar, however, so far from doing so, answered with a strong defence of the anti-Maimunist standpoint. He charged Maimonides with trying to reconcile two things which were in their nature irreconcilable, Greek philosophy and Judaism. He went on to argue that Philosophy, which is built on reasoning, can easily fall into false conclusions, and cannot therefore be associated with the certainty offered by revelation. Maimonides' method of reducing the miracles to natural phenomena was against the plain sense of the Scriptural text. Maimonides had professed his ability, in case of need, to explain away the doctrine of *creatio ex nihilo* so plainly indicated in the Scripture, although on it depended the sanctity of the Sabbath. The *Guide* certainly contained some excellent ideas, but with them others which were dangerous, and it would have been better if it had never been written. Maimonides' admirers placed him above the prophets, which was not right, and would have been displeasing to himself. The chief blame, however, attached to Samuel ibn Tibbon on account of his translation of the *Guide* into Hebrew, which had helped to disseminate more widely its dangerous ideas.

In spite of the support of such men as Alfachar, Nachmanides and Meir Abulafia, the cause of Solomon gradually lost ground. If the teaching of Maimonides led to religious laxity, its rejection was likely to lead to anthropomorphic conceptions of God, which in the eyes of the enlightened Spanish Jews was worse. The leading anti-Maimunists themselves became suspect, and David ben Saul felt compelled to write a defence of himself and his teacher against such a charge.

Solomon commenced to feel himself isolated, and in order to retrieve his position resorted to a procedure the gravity of which he does not seem to have appreciated. He invited the Dominican friars, to whose hands Pope Gregory IX had just entrusted the Inquisition, to burn publicly the heretical books of Maimonides. The Dominicans were only too ready to do so, not only for Solomon's sake but for their own, since, as it seems, the *Guide* had already been translated into Latin, and it was therefore capable of being as harmful to Christianity as to Judaism. A public burning of some works of Maimonides took place, according to report, in Montpellier, and soon after a similar one, instigated by Jonah Gerondi, in Paris.

The effect of this proceeding, as might have been expected, was to create a strong reaction in favour of Maimonides. Many who were inclined to side with Solomon and Jonah Gerondi were indignant at the lengths to which they had gone to attain their end. Nachmanides and Meir Abulafia were reduced to silence, and Alfachar felt compelled to apologize for Solomon's behaviour. King James of Aragon, to whose domain Montpellier belonged, put a stop to the persecution of the Maimunists in that city. This was the last of any attempts in Spain or Provence to prevent the study of Maimonides or of philosophy in general. Henceforth the zealots for moral reform eschewed this particular weapon.

The seal was set on the victory of the Maimunists by the

open recantation of their most formidable opponent, Jonah of Gerona. In 1242 the Dominicans, whose assistance he had invoked against Maimonides, publicly burnt his beloved Talmud in Paris. He saw in this a divine punishment for the part he had played in the burning of the works of Maimonides. Filled with remorse he made open repentance in the synagogue and declared his intention of going on a pilgrimage to the grave of Maimonides in Tiberias in Palestine and seeking his pardon. Circumstances prevented him from carrying out his design, but thenceforth he always spoke of Maimonides with the greatest reverence; and his example had a powerful effect not only in Spain and Provence, but also in Northern France.

Half a century after the ban of Solomon of Montpellier history repeated itself in a precisely similar proceeding in another part of the world. Germany was at this time an important centre of Talmudical study, with Rabbis even more uncompromising than those of France had been in the days of Jonah of Gerona. One of these, Moses Taku of Regensburg, roundly condemned not only Maimonides, but also Saadiah, for having introduced the study of philosophy into Judaism. An even more bitter enemy of philosophy was a Jew from the Rhineland of French origin named Solomon Petit, whose opposition, however, was inspired by a zeal rather for mysticism than for the Talmud.

Petit settled in Acre in Palestine, then a centre of Jewish mysticism, and there formed a plan for placing Maimonides and the study of philosophy once more under the ban. In 1289 he went to Germany and found there considerable support. From Germany he went to Italy, where Jewish studies had also revived of late, but here he had little success. On returning to Acre, he induced the leaders of the community there to condemn Maimonides's *Guide* and to pronounce a ban against all who should occupy themselves with it.

From this point events took a different course from that of fifty years before. Solomon Petit failed to rally to his side anyone of the standing of Nachmanides or Jonah of Gerona. Hillel of Verona, the leading Jewish scholar of Italy and a great admirer of Maimonides, wrote a letter to David Maimuni, a grandson of Maimonides and head of the Jewish community in Egypt, suggesting that the matter should be laid before a Rabbinical synod to be convened in Alexandria, by the decision of which all should abide. David, however, refused to pay Petit so great a compliment. Instead he sent a circular letter to all the chief communities of the Orient, calling on them to defend the honour of his grandfather against his bigoted opponents. He received overwhelming support. Petit and his colleagues were threatened from many sides with the ban, and were reduced to complete silence.

Although the study of the *Guide* was thus vindicated in all parts of the Jewish world, the anti-Maimunist spirit still persisted, and it soon led to a conflict which came near to reopening the whole question. Towards the end of the thirteenth century a fanatical Talmudist named Abba Mari, in Perpignan, near Montpellier, started a movement for suppressing the pursuit of secular knowledge, and the reading of profane works in general, among the Jews. He appealed to Solomon ben Adret, the Rabbi of Barcelona, who at that time enjoyed an almost undisputed authority in religious matters, to forbid the reading of such works by Jewish youth up to the age of thirty. He was strenuously opposed by Jacob ibn Tibbon (known in Christian circles as Profatius or Don Profiat), of Montpellier, who had himself translated Euclid and other scientific works into Hebrew. Ibn Tibbon also addressed himself to Solomon ben Adret, adducing the example of King Solomon who "spoke on all trees from the cedars of Lebanon to the hyssop on the wall," and pointed out that it was very difficult to take up the study of a new subject after the age of thirty.

A heated controversy ensued, similar to that which had convulsed the Jewries of Spain and Provence in 1232, and though the name of Maimonides was not mentioned everyone knew that he was the real object of the attack. The lead in the campaign against profane knowledge was taken by the famous German Talmudist Asher ben Yechiel ("Asheri"), who had been driven from Germany and had become Rabbi of Toledo. At Asheri's instigation in July 1305, Solomon ben Adret pronounced a ban on anyone who should read any scientific work whether in Hebrew or in the original language, and he solemnly cursed those who, in order to reconcile religion and philosophy, interpreted the Bible allegorically—a method which had come greatly into fashion recently.

Jacob ibn Tibbon and his party refused to bow to this order. They issued in Montpellier a counter-ban against any who from religious scruples should prevent their sons of whatever age from studying any science in whatever language, against those who uttered any word of condemnation or disrespect against the great Maimonides, and against those who should curse any religious writer on account of his philosophical method. They were supported by a young Hebrew poet of repute named Jedaiah of Bezières (Bedaresi) who sent Adret a letter in defence of Maimonides concluding with the following words: "We cannot give up the pursuit of (secular) knowledge, it is the breath of our life. Even if Joshua were to arise and forbid it to us, we could not listen to him. For it is recommended to us by an authority who outweighs you all, Maimonides."

The dispute was cut short almost immediately afterwards by the expulsion of the Jews from France in 1306. In practice the Jews of Spain continued to study philosophy and secular sciences, while those of Germany and, later, of Poland confined themselves almost exclusively to the study of the Talmud and its allied subjects.

When the Jews were expelled from Spain at the end of the fifteenth century, they carried with them the Maimonidean spirit of free inquiry into the Ottoman Empire and Italy, and, later, into the Netherlands. In the Ottoman Empire the spark naturally soon faded away, but in Italy and Holland it was kept alive, though with diminished lustre, and it smouldered on even in Germany until it was rekindled to a new brilliance by the breath of European culture.

CHAPTER VI

CABBALISTS AND ANTI-CABBALISTS

If after the death of Maimonides the Jews of Spain and Southern France began to turn away from the study of philosophy, the reason was not only that they saw in it a danger to the authority of the Talmud. There was also another reason which, at first subsidiary, came in course of time to be decisive. This was that numbers of Jews believed themselves to have found a source of enlightenment superior to philosophy on the very questions for the answer to which men turned to philosophy, such as the nature of God, the relation of God to the universe, the character of the soul and its ultimate destination, and so forth. This new source was more akin to revelation than to logic; it gave certainty where philosophy gave only probability, and therefore enabled its devotees to dispense entirely with the latter.

This quasi revelation was called Cabbalah, a name which now becomes common for the first time in this sense. The word Cabbalah means literally "receiving," and the reason why it was applied to the new doctrine is nowhere clearly stated. Since, however, it was distinctly mystical in character, we may surmise that one reason was that it was to be "received" by the learner as a kind of illumination, while another may have been that those who partook of this illumination were "received" into a circle of the elect.

The first exponent of Cabbalah known to us by name was one Isaac the Blind, of Posquières, an opponent of Maimonides at the end of the twelfth century. Of Isaac's teaching little is known, and the first authoritative exposition of Cabbalah comes from the works of a disciple of his named Ezra ben Solomon, one of the principal figures in a group of mystics which flourished at Gerona in Spain. Ezra taught that nothing can be predi-

CABBALISTS AND ANTI-CABBALISTS 69

cated of God as such, who is therefore to be designated *En Sof*, "without end" or "definition." Between God and the universe there are certain intermediaries called *Sefiroth* (lit. "countings"; sing. *sefirah*), to which the universe owes its existence. The Sefiroth are ten in number and form a hierarchy, the highest emanating directly from the En Sof and the rest from one another; and each possesses its own distinct range of creative power.

To this doctrine were added two others—whether by Ezra himself or his successors—of equally fundamental importance for the Cabbalistic doctrine. One was that the tenth or lowest Sefirah not only creates the soul of man but in some way permeates it and imparts to it something of its own essence. The other was that in the linking of the soul with the Sefirah and of the Sefiroth with the En Sof a capital part is played by the sacred name of God, the Tetragrammaton.

The Cabbalistic doctrine bears an obvious resemblance to the teaching of the Neo-Platonists and of some of the Gnostics of the early Christian centuries. That it was consciously taken from these sources is possible but by no means certain. It is equally possible that both were derived from older sources. Certain it is that the Cabbalists themselves claimed for their doctrine a high antiquity, ascribing it to the prophets, if not to Moses himself, though its first exponents admitted that they could find no clear indication of it in the Pentateuch. According to them it had been transmitted for generations as a secret lore in the East, but how it had come to the West they did not explain.

The Cabbalah rapidly gained adherents in Spain and Provence, especially among Jews of philosophic temperament who were yet jealous for the honour and authority of the Talmud. Conspicuous among these was the great Talmudical scholar and anti-Maimunist, Moses ben Nachman (Nachmani) of Gerona (*vide* p. 63). Nachmani greatly furthered the spread of the Cabbalah, not only by his example but also by finding warrant for it in the Pentateuch. In his commentary on the Pentateuch published in 1265 he proclaimed that the Law of Moses was full of mysteries and discovered hints of Cabbalistic doctrines in various passages in the text.

The task of basing the Cabbalah on the Pentateuch was carried out in greater detail by a book which appeared about thirty years after the death of Nachmani, under the title of *Midrash of Rabbi Simon ben Yochai*. This book was in form a midrashic commentary on the Pentateuch, that is, it professed to record the biblical expositions of certain ancient Rabbinical authorities, the chief of whom was Simon ben Yochai, a Palestinian scholar of the second century.

What gave this midrash its distinctive character was the fact that its expositions were largely Cabbalistic. This was especially the case with the commentary on the first two chapters of Genesis, into which the basic doctrines of the Cabbalah were read with great elaboration. From the fact that the work opened with a quotation of Daniel xii, 3: "And they that are wise shall shine as the brightness (Heb. *zohar*) of the firmament," the work came to be generally known by the name of Zohar.

Besides the Cabbalah proper the Zohar contained much mystical teaching of a more popular kind which had long been current in the Jewish people, some of it in writing. Much of this was probably derived from schools of mystics and pietists which had flourished in Germany even before the rise of the Provençal Cabbalah, and which in turn had sprung from earlier schools in Palestine and Mesopotamia. Thus the Zohar described minutely the heavenly Paradise where the soul originated and the earthly Paradise where it waited for its union with the body. It explained exactly how the soul came to be joined with the body and how it was parted from it again, and what became of it after death. It also described in detail the circumstances in which the Messiah would appear, and provided data for calculating the date of his coming.

Thus the Zohar, like the Talmud, had a popular as well as an intellectual appeal. Its theosophy and cosmogony were no doubt "caviare to the general," but its descriptions of the "future world," its angelology, and its apocalyptic visions, were well calculated to capture the imagination of the masses. They supplemented the scattered hints of the *haggadah* on these subjects, by which the mind of the people had already been well prepared for their reception.

The Zohar was actually published by a Spanish scholar named Moses ben Shemtob of Leon (c. 1250-1305), who, however, gave it out as the work of R. Simon ben Yochai himself. He affirmed that it had been secretly preserved in the East, and had come into his hands somewhat accidentally. It was at once denounced by more than one scholar as a fabrication. Others, however, especially among those who were already Cabbalists, accepted Moses de Leon's story at its face value, and, regarding the Zohar as the authentic work of Simon ben Yochai, treated it with the utmost reverence. The question of its authenticity soon became inextricably mixed up with that of the value and truth of the Cabbalah, and remained so until comparatively recent times.

The Cabbalah—and with it the Zohar—appealed primarily to those who at all costs demanded a faith, and who in order to obtain such faith were not averse to doing violence to reason. Conversely it repelled the Aristotelians, to whom reason was sacrosanct. This was the chief line of cleavage for many centuries between Cabbalists and anti-Cabbalists. A typical example of the latter was the well-known Italian philosophic writer, Elia del Medigo, at the end of the fifteenth century. As, however, the authority of Aristotle gradually declined both among Jews and non-Jews, the opposition to the Cabbalah on this ground became more and more feeble. In 1638 the noted Italian Jewish scholar and rationalist, Leon de Modena, wrote a scathing denunciation of the Zohar as a mass of nonsense, but it was a lone voice, and he did not even venture to publish it in his lifetime.

With the Talmud also the Zohar was in many respects at variance, hardly less so than Maimonides, though of course in a different way. On the subject of the unity of God it was no less equivocal than he had been on the *creatio ex nihilo*. It gave reasons for the precepts which were as little consonant with the Talmud as his had been. It spoke at times with great scorn of the study of the Mishnah in comparison with that of the Cabbalah. On some ceremonial points it prescribed rules different from those of orthodox Judaism.

For these reasons there were always Talmudical scholars who looked on it with suspicion. In 1558 a number of Rabbis tried to prevent it from being printed on the ground that it was a heretical and dangerous work. For the majority of Talmudists, however, these considerations were outweighed by the fact that it was a valuable ally in the fight against Maimunist rationalism (*vide* Chapter v). The name of Rabbi Simon ben Yochai attached to the Zohar stamped it as authoritative, and gradually it came to be venerated by the majority of the Jewish people as a holy work. Through its influence the Cabbalah, and Jewish mysticism in general, grew to be widely regarded as an integral part of the Mosaic revelation, analogous to the Oral Law, being to faith and belief what the Oral Law was to practice and conduct.

In the middle of the sixteenth century the Cabbalah obtained a kind of official recognition as an integral part of Rabbinic Judaism. The chief centre of Jewish learning at that time was Safed in Palestine, where Talmud and Zohar were studied with equal zest. Here lived Rabbi Joseph Caro, the great authority on Jewish law, whose code was accepted by all sections of the Jewish people (*vide* p. 56). Caro was himself a mystic, and among his disciples and closest friends was Moses Cordoveiro (1522–1576), who in the sphere of Cabbalah was reckoned as great an authority as Caro on Jewish law. The rest of the Safed circle were the disciples alike of Caro and of Cordoveiro, and looked on the Cabbalah as the indispensable complement of the law.

From this union of Cabbalah and law emerged an interesting variant of Rabbinic Judaism. One of the disciples of Cordoveiro named Isaac Luria (1534–1572) developed in a special manner the Cabbalistic theory of the relation of the soul to God. In his opinion it was not sufficient merely to perform the commandments; they should be performed with what he called *kavvanah* ("intention" or "concentration"), in such a way, that is, as to become the instruments for uniting the soul with God.

To attain to this *kavvanah* he introduced various new practices, mostly of an ascetic character, and gave to others a symbolical significance. Luria gathered round himself a band of disciples, and his ideas and way of life, known as the "Lurian Cabbalah," gained many adherents both in Palestine and other countries.

CABBALISTS AND ANTI-CABBALISTS 73

The symbolism of Luria was in itself only a refinement on Talmudic Judaism and at no point came into conflict with it. It paved the way, however, for another movement which contained grave if hidden dangers for Rabbinic Judaism, and ultimately came into violent conflict with it. From symbolism it was only a short step to occultism, a pursuit which had always had its devotees among the Jews. Hitherto, however, it had been kept within bounds which rendered it comparatively harmless; it was now to be practised on a scale which convulsed the whole Jewish world and caused no small commotion in the Christian world also.

Jewish occultism consisted intrinsically in the attribution of thaumaturgic or magic powers to the letters of the Hebrew alphabet, especially those composing the holy name of God, the Tetragrammaton. Belief in such powers was very ancient among the Jews, and we find instances in the Talmud of their use for faith-healing and similar purposes.

When the Cabbalah came into vogue in the thirteenth century, it was brought into connection with these practices through the importance which it attached to the Tetragrammaton; and these were also designated Cabbalah. Thus the Cabbalah was divided into two kinds, speculative and practical. Considerable space was devoted in the Zohar to the lore of the practical Cabbalah; and though it was frowned on by Cordoveiro and no doubt other thinkers of his stamp, it was placed by less critical readers of the Zohar on the same level as the speculative Cabbalah.

Among these uncritical readers was one who was destined to make occultism for a short time the dominant force in the Jewish religion—the celebrated pseudo-Messiah Sabbatai (more correctly Shabbetai) Zevi, the son of a small trader in Smyrna, to whom he was born in 1626. From his early youth Sabbatai immersed himself in the study of the Zohar and adopted the Lurian asceticism in all its rigour. It was a time when millenary aspirations were much in the air both among Jews and among Christians, and the young Sabbatai, being of a visionary disposition, conceived the idea that he was the Messiah who was destined to restore the Jewish people to its land and independence.

From the Zohar he had learnt the Cabbalistic use of the Tetragrammaton, and this was to be his great instrument for carrying out his designs; he certainly seems to have had no other Messianic qualifications. He first declared himself to be the Messiah at the age of twenty-two, to a chosen band of confidants. His activities aroused the suspicions of the Rabbis of Smyrna, who were afraid that he might embroil them with the Turkish authorities; and accordingly they placed him under the ban and eventually in 1651 or 1654 procured his banishment from Smyrna.

Going to Egypt, he secured there the support of a wealthy banker named Raphael Joseph Chelebi. Even more important to him was the accession of a young man named Nathan Levi of Gaza in Palestine, commonly known as Nathan Ghazzati, who espoused his cause with all the fervour of a prophet and sought by every means to gain adherents for him. Instigated by Chelebi and Nathan Ghazzati, Sabbatai in 1665 openly proclaimed himself the Messiah at Salonica. Large numbers of Jews in the Turkish Empire at once admitted his claim, and those who questioned it were reduced to silence.

His fame soon spread abroad and he was acclaimed by the whole community of Amsterdam, then the most influential and the most enlightened in Western Europe. Many Christians also watched his progress with warm sympathy. The only voice of any influence raised against him among the Jews was that of Jacob Sasportas, the Rabbi of Hamburg, whose warnings, however, fell on deaf ears.

Sabbatai for a time continued to observe the rigorous practices of his youth. Gradually, however, some of his followers, in the certainty that the national deliverance was at hand, threw off the restraints of Jewish law and indulged in all kinds of excesses which greatly scandalized the pious, without, however, seriously shaking them in their allegiance to Sabbatai himself.

In 1666, which according to the calculations of the Sabbatians was to be the year of destiny, the Turkish authorities considered that the agitation was becoming dangerous and threw Sabbatai into prison. As the ferment among the Jews still continued, Sabbatai later in the year was brought before the Sultan and charged with high treason. Finding his incanta-

CABBALISTS AND ANTI-CABBALISTS 75

tions of no avail in this predicament, he saved his life by adopting Islam. This at last opened the eyes of the mass of the Jews to the falsity of his Messianic pretensions, and disabused many, especially in the West, of their belief in the practical Cabbalah.

Among the masses, however, this belief died very hard. Large numbers of Jews were still not convinced that Sabbatai Zevi had not possessed miraculous powers, and in secret continued to show their faith in him by using amulets containing his name to which they attributed magical potency for the curing of disease and other purposes. For a hundred years after the death of Sabbatai the more enlightened Rabbis of Germany and Poland waged an unceasing war against the use of these amulets. Nor was it only the ignorant who were suspect.

About the year 1750 Jacob Emden, the Rabbi of Altona, accused Jonathan Eibeschütz, the Rabbi of Prague, of writing amulets containing the name of Sabbatai Zevi. Eibeschütz vehemently denied the charge and a quarrel broke out between the two Rabbis—who were among the greatest Talmudical authorities of their time—which convulsed the whole of Jewry.

Through his controversy with Eibeschütz, Jacob Emden was led to subject the Zohar to a critical examination, the results of which he published in 1763. His conclusion was that part of it went back to the Gaonic age and contained Cabbalistic traditions of great antiquity, while the rest belonged to the Spanish age and might in part be the composition of Moses de Leon. Most modern scholars agree with Emden in regarding the Zohar as a compilation of elements belonging to widely distant periods, though on the age of the Cabbalah itself there is still great difference of opinion.

Alongside of those Jews who still cherished the memory of Sabbatai Zevi there were a number who continued to hope for his reappearance as Messiah and to organize their lives accordingly. At the time when he embraced Islam a number of his adherents had followed his example, and after his death these organized themselves into a sect which while conforming outwardly to Mohammedanism retained a number of Jewish practices and looked forward to a redemption by a resurrected

Sabbatai Zevi. They were known to the Turks as Dönmeh ("apostates"), but called themselves "believers," and in spite of occasional persecution by the authorities and ostracism by the Jewish community they survived in small numbers into the present century.

During the hundred years following the apostasy of Sabbatai Zevi a number of men appeared in various parts who claimed a kind of apostolic succession to him and set themselves up as leaders. The last and most prominent of these was one Jacob Frank, of Podolia, a Polish province on the borders of the Ottoman Empire.

About 1755 Frank proclaimed himself to be a kind of avatar of Sabbatai Zevi and his successor in the Messiahship, and he gathered round himself a considerable following among the crypto-Sabbatians of Podolia. Frank went further than Sabbatai by decreeing the abrogation of the Talmud and the substitution of the Zohar as the basis of Jewish teaching; and his followers, like some of the Sabbatians before them, showed a total disregard of Jewish law and morality. They made themselves so objectionable to the Rabbis that the latter had to call in the aid of the civil authorities to keep the new heresy in check; and eventually, to avoid further persecution, Frank with some thousands of his followers embraced Christianity.

The Sabbatian and Frankist movements showed that the Zohar was a dangerous edge tool which, while it could kindle religious enthusiasm, might also lead to dangerous excesses. After the criticisms of Emden it lost its prestige in Western Europe. In Eastern Europe and in the Orient, however, it continued to be studied alongside of the Talmud and to be regarded with equal veneration. And it was still to prove itself capable of inspiring a new movement which challenged the predominance of the Talmud almost as sharply as Sabbatianism had done.

CHAPTER VII

CHASSIDIM AND MITHNAGEDIM

THE failure of the Sabbatian movement to restore the Jews to their own land gave a heightened importance to the spiritual leaders of the people in exile. Hitherto the belief in the early appearance of the Messiah had been a powerful force—perhaps the most powerful—in keeping the mass of the Jews true to their religion and restraining them from adopting Christianity. That hope still remained, but it had been greatly weakened by the Sabbatian debacle, and a greater responsibility was in consequence thrown upon the Rabbis for maintaining the morale of the people.

Since about the middle of the fourteenth century most of the larger Jewish communities had adopted the custom of appointing a salaried official as their spiritual leader. In Poland this official came to be known commonly as the *Rav* (plu. *Rabbonim*, lit. "master") of the community. Naturally he had to be a *talmid chakham*, a man well versed in the Talmud and Jewish learning generally, and as such he was addressed as "Rabbi" (*vide supra*, p. 34). Hence it is usual in English to call these officials Rabbis, like the authors of the Talmud, who, however, were not salaried officials of the communities. The chief function of the official Rabbi was to study the Talmud himself and to encourage and assist the study of the *torah* in his community. In Poland, where the largest number of Jews were settled and where they had the highest measure of autonomy, *torah* for the Rabbi meant principally the Talmud, and especially its legal portions.

In the middle of the eighteenth century, about the same time that Jacob Frank repudiated the authority of the Talmud, the spiritual leadership of the Rabbis was contested in a different way from another quarter. This new challenge, like that of Sabbatai Zevi and Frank, was also inspired by the Zohar, but in a somewhat more indirect fashion.

Running through the Zohar is the idea that whatever happens in the earthly or "lower" world is prefigured in the heavenly or "upper" world. This idea is found in various Oriental creeds, but it was given a new turn by the Jewish Cabbalists. They taught that the *tzaddik*, or perfectly righteous man, is a link between the upper and lower worlds, and is able on the one hand by his personality to bring his fellow-men into communion with God, and on the other hand by his prayers and righteous actions to influence the course of events in the "upper world." Simon ben Yochai, the reputed author of the Zohar, was to them the type of the *tzaddik* of this kind.

In an obscure village of Bukowina, about the year 1700, there was born a child, Israel, son of Eliezer, who was destined to give this doctrine a new importance in Jewish society. In his early years Israel was a Hebrew teacher, and while still young he obtained the reputation of being a *baal-shem* (lit. "Master of the Name"), that is, one who by means of a cabbalistic use of the name of God or of angels could effect cures or cast out evil spirits.

On account of this activity he came to be commonly known as Israel Baal-shem.[1] In fact, however, unlike Sabbatai Zevi, he took little interest in occultism. Certainly he preferred the study of the Zohar to that of the Talmud, in which he acquired no great proficiency. But the part of the Zohar's teaching which particularly attracted him was that relating to the *tzaddik*, and he gradually came to regard himself as fulfilling that character. This notion was strengthened by a sojourn which he made in a lonely part of the Carpathian mountains, where he earned a scanty living as a lime-burner and had ample time for meditation and prayer.

After reaching the age of forty, Israel Baal-shem decided that it was time to reveal himself to the world in his true character. He chose as the sphere of his work the Jewish com-

---

[1] In Jewish writings he is commonly referred to as "the Besht," a name formed from the initial letters of Baal Shem Tob ("Master of the Good Name").

CHASSIDIM AND MITHNAGEDIM 79

munities of Podolia and Wallachia, in southern Poland, not far from his own birthplace. The Jews here were in the mass much less educated than those of northern Poland. Most of them knew enough Hebrew to say their prayers, but not enough to study the Talmud with any profit. They felt that their spiritual needs were being neglected by the Talmudical scholars, whose arid discussions on fine points of law they were incapable of following. They were lost sheep of Israel who were waiting for a shepherd to lead them back to the fold.

For the next twenty years, up to his death in 1762, Israel Baal-shem went about among the Jews of southern Poland, instilling into them by means of informal conversations the ideas which had come to him from his meditations in the lonely Carpathian forests. He did not proclaim himself as a *tzaddik*, but rather allowed this to appear from his conduct and teaching. Certainly if there was one man more than another in the Jewish people who deserved the title, it was he.

Though greatly inferior to the Rabbis in learning, he was greatly superior to many of them in character. He was entirely devoid both of arrogance and of envy, the two besetting sins of the Polish Rabbis of the time. He associated with the common people on equal terms and treated them like friends and brothers. In his teaching he constantly laid stress on the omnipresence of God, of which in the eyes of his followers he himself was the living proof. He proclaimed to them that the chosen instrument for communing with God was prayer when offered in a condition of ecstasy, and he showed them how to work themselves up into this state. In the sphere of ethics he attached particular importance to the virtues of brotherly love and mutual help and forbearance, and of cheerfulness under all conditions, however adverse.

To the unsophisticated Jews of southern Poland this presentation of Judaism proved highly attractive. More and more of them came to regard Israel as their teacher and to reverence him as a *tzaddik*, so that eventually he found himself at the head of a large body of adherents. Nor was his following confined entirely to the uneducated. About 1750 he was joined by a learned Talmudist named Ber of Mizriez (Meseritz) who had won great repute as a *Maggid*, or itinerant preacher. Ber became his lieutenant and set himself to win over the youth of the Rabbinical colleges, not without a considerable measure of success.

Israel Baal-shem's activities among the Jews of southern Poland show a striking resemblance to those of Jesus of Nazareth among the Jews of Palestine. Like Jesus he sought to bring a message of comfort and edification to the ignorant and illiterate among his brethren whose spiritual welfare was neglected by the authorized teachers of religion. Like Jesus too, he sought to achieve this end by giving them an emotional approach to God. But whereas Jesus claimed to hold in his hand the key of entry to the kingdom of heaven, Israel Baal-shem did not pretend to do more than make his fellow-Jews aware of the presence of God upon earth. This, however, was sufficient to secure for him an ascendancy over his followers almost as great as had been exercised by Jesus over his. He was all but deified by them, especially after his death, and like Jesus he became the subject of a mass of legends from which it is very difficult to pick out the actual facts of his life.

Israel's followers were called *Chassidim* (Pietists), and they formed themselves into communities permeated with a strong spirit of brotherhood, rich and poor, learned and unlearned, mixing in them on perfectly equal terms. So long as Israel lived, there was no conflict between the *Chassidim* and the rest of the Jews. Israel himself kept on good terms with the Rabbis, who regarded his movement with rather good-natured contempt. After all there was nothing in it which was actually contrary to Jewish law, and it might be of benefit to the *am ha-aretz* (lit. "people of the earth," i.e. illiterate).

After Israel's death, Ber of Meseritz proclaimed himself leader of the movement and the Baal-shem's successor as the *tzaddik*. Whether Israel had actually nominated him before his death we do not know, but at any rate his leadership was generally accepted. Ber adopted a much more active proselytizing policy than his predecessor. He was assisted by a band of ardent disciples, men of learning and ability, who went further and further afield to win adherents for the Baal-shem. Thanks to their efforts the Chassidic movement soon became a power in southern Poland.

Ber of Meseritz was of a somewhat different type from his Master. While genuinely pious and devoted to his teacher, he was at the same time ambitious and eager for power, and he sought to use the Chassidic movement for gratifying these passions. For this purpose he introduced the doctrine—which probably never crossed the mind of Israel himself—that not only was the latter himself a *tzaddik*, but that he was the one source and fountain-head of *tzaddikism* for his own and future generations.

Those therefore on whom the Baal-shem's mantle had fallen—like himself and other of Israel's immediate disciples—became *tzaddikim* by a kind of apostolic succession, and were entitled to transmit their office to their disciples and descendants by hereditary right. Ber also somewhat changed the relation of the *tzaddik* to the community. Not only did he emphasize the importance of the *tzaddik* as an intermediary between man and God, but he proclaimed that in virtue of this function it was the bounden duty of his fellow-Jews—in fact, their first duty—to love, honour and support him.

Along with other more commendable parts of Ber's teaching, the credulous Jews of South Poland swallowed this also. They contributed liberally to the maintenance of the various *tzaddikim*, and paid them the same homage as they had paid to the Baal-shem. The first generation of *tzaddikim* on the whole followed in the footsteps of their Master. They genuinely sought to promote the moral if not intellectual welfare of their followers, especially to instil in them the virtues of brotherhood and cheerfulness, and to rouse them to ecstatic prayer. But in later generations many were not proof against the seductions of power, and while maintaining their hold over their followers by various kinds of charlatanism, took advantage of their hero-worship for their own personal enrichment; some of them kept a kind of court where they lived in almost princely state, and to which the faithful resorted on set occasions to pay their homage to the Master and be entertained by him with both physical and spiritual nourishment.

The *tzaddik* was familiarly known to his followers as the *Rebbe*, to distinguish him from the ordinary Rabbi, whom he resembled in being the spiritual head of his community and who was usually called Rav (Master). His chief occupation, like that of the Rabbi, was to teach the *torah*, but he meant something considerably different by that word. To the Rabbi the *torah* meant primarily the *halachah* and *hagadah* of the Talmud and the Midrash. These were taught also by the *tzaddik*, but in a somewhat perfunctory fashion.

What the *tzaddik* understood by *torah* was primarily the teaching of the Baal-shem. Israel himself had left nothing in writing, but Ber of Meseritz had collected many of his sayings and reduced them to writing, and by adding a good deal of his own had produced a kind of Chassidic doctrine, which was further elaborated by other leaders of the movement, the whole being attributed to the Baal-shem himself. This work, and with it another containing all sorts of marvellous legends about the Baal-shem, became the accepted text-books of Chassidism and the staple of the *torah* of the Rebbes. The Rebbe's expositions of the Bible and Talmud were suited to the intellectual level of his audience, and were capable of any degree of bizarrerie in the attempt to find support for Chassidic doctrines.

This essentially popular teaching, with its emotional appeal, exactly met the needs of the Jewish masses of southern Poland, utterly unable as they were to appreciate either the hair-splitting dialectics of the Talmud or the recondite metaphysics of the Zohar. In consequence, before long Chassidism became the dominant form of Judaism in that region, and its adherents were able to stigmatize those who rejected the Baal-shem as *mithnagedim* (opposers), a name which has clung to them to this day. Nor did its proselytizing zeal stop at this point. It was carried into northern Poland and Lithuania and won many adherents there also.

In these districts, however, the opposition to Chassidism was much stronger. The intellectual level of the Jews, especially in Lithuania, was much higher, and most of them had at least a smattering of Talmud. They had to be appealed to through their intellect and not through their emotions. Hence the *Tzaddikim* who came into these parts were also of a different type. They were men of great Talmudical learning and more akin to the "opposition" Rabbis than to their fellow-Tzaddikim

CHASSIDIM AND MITHNAGEDIM 83

in southern Poland; in fact, they differed from the former not so much in accepting the teaching of the Baal-shem—of which they can hardly have had any great opinion—as in ranking the Zohar above the Talmud, though they held the latter work also in high esteem.

Conspicuous among them were two scholars, Mendel of Vitebsk and Shneur Zalman of Ladi (1746–1812), who were highly respected by the Mithnagedim as well as by the Chassidim. The latter wrote a philosophical essay in Hebrew on the nature of the soul. His followers were known as the *ChaBaD*, a name formed from the initial letters of the three Hebrew words *CHokhmah* (wisdom), *Binah* (understanding), and *Da'ath* (knowledge), which they took as their watchwords.

The spread of Chassidism was viewed with deep apprehension by the Rabbis of Lithuania, who saw in it a danger to the study of the Talmud. On its first appearance in Lithuania they made vigorous efforts to suppress it. Among other things they called to their aid a man whose name was a household word among the Jews of Poland and who commanded the deepest respect of all sections, Elijah ben Solomon of Wilna, commonly known as Elijah Wilna (1729–1797). At an early age Elijah had been acknowledged as the foremost Talmudical scholar of his day, and he had made himself equally master of the Zohar and of most branches of Hebrew literature.

He was remarkable not only for the extent of his learning, but for his power of arranging it logically and imparting it methodically. He did more than any other scholar had done for generations to bring order into the study and teaching of Hebrew literature, and in this respect was the absolute antithesis of the Rebbes, to most of whom order itself was anathema. He was now for the first and only time in his life induced to emerge from his retirement, in order to combat the danger with which the mass emotionalism of Chassidism threatened his favourite study.

With the concurrence of Elijah Wilna the Rabbis of Lithuania in 1772 issued a ban against the Chassidim, which they caused to be published far and wide. Their ostensible ground was that the Chassidim, in order to facilitate their own peculiar method of praying, had made certain alterations in the established form of prayer, and also in the orthodox ritual.[1] But their real reason was the undisguised hostility shown by the *Tzaddikim* to the teachers of the Talmud, and the contemptuous way in which they spoke of the Talmud itself in comparison with the teaching of the Baal-shem.

At one time the ban, or excommunication, had been a powerful weapon in the hands of Talmudical scholars for upholding their authority and dignity. It had been really effective in placing those on whom it was imposed outside the pale of Jewish society for a longer or shorter period. By now it had lost most of its terrors, and served as little more than a demonstration. But the signature of Elijah Wilna produced a powerful effect on public opinion. If the Chassidim themselves still persisted in their errors, those who might otherwise have joined them refrained.

A bitter controversy broke out between the *Tzaddikim* and the Rabbis, which lasted for the remainder of Elijah's life, and in 1782 Elijah saw himself obliged to join the Rabbis in issuing a fresh ban, in which this time Shneur Zalman of Ladi was also included. The quarrel went on unabated for several years. By the time of Elijah's death, however, in 1797, it had become clear that the Chassidim could not hope to make any further progress in Lithuania and White Russia. On the other hand the Rabbis were unable to recover any of the ground they had lost in southern Poland, and here the Chassidim remained dominant.

Soon afterwards Chassidism in Galicia, its chief stronghold, had to face a more formidable enemy in the new "enlightenment," or *Haskalah* movement (*vide* Chapter viii) which had come in from Germany. The younger *maskilim*—many of whom had sprung from Chassidic homes—saw in Chassidim the worst enemy of enlightenment, and turned against it the keenest shafts of their irony and ridicule. In their detestation of its obscurantism and superstition they overlooked its redeeming features and gave it even a worse name than it deserved. For Chassidism even in its degeneracy—nor was it

---

[1] Actually the Chassidim went no further than to adopt certain practices from the "Sephardim," the Jews of Spanish descent in Southern Europe, who were also orthodox, though in a slightly different way from the Jews of Poland and Germany.

everywhere degenerate—preserved intact two of the most precious qualities of its founder—the feeling of brotherly affection towards fellow-Jews, and cheerfulness in adversity based on a living faith. In virtue of these qualities it succeeded in retaining a strong hold on Polish Jewry almost up to the present day.

PART II
MODERN TRENDS

CHAPTER VIII
THE ENLIGHTENMENT MOVEMENT

IN the teaching of the Rabbis it was customary to identify *torah* with wisdom as the highest goal of man's intellectual strivings. The study of the *torah* if carried far enough would lead to the attainment of wisdom; and conversely the Jew who desired to attain wisdom would seek it through the medium of the study of the *torah*. This idea was accepted by practically all Jews, up to the middle of the eighteenth century. There might be differences of opinion as to the precise part of the *torah* literature in which wisdom was to be found, whether the Bible, or the Talmud, or the Zohar. But that the secret was contained in one or other of these was never denied. The one man who did openly deny it, Baruch Spinoza, was unable to remain within the community.

This idea had not prevented the Arabic-speaking Jews in the golden age of Arabic learning from prosecuting with ardour the study of Arabic literature and seeking from it instruction of all kinds. The reason was that they were able to turn all this instruction to account for a better understanding of the *torah* itself, which still remained for them the path to wisdom. But after the end of the Arabic period the Jewish intelligentsia on the whole made little effort to acquaint itself with the new culture which arose in Europe after the Renaissance. For one thing the Jews had now a vast literature of their own which was ample enough to absorb all their energies. Facilities for prosecuting other studies were also lacking. For whatever reason, it became exceptional for a Jew to take up seriously any non-Jewish branch of study, with the exception of medicine.

It was this difference in culture which prevented the Jews from even commencing to Europeanize themselves. Difference of religion kept them apart from their non-Jewish surroundings;

but difference of culture made them something different in themselves. This was the case to some extent even with those Jews—and there were such, especially in England and France—who had more of non-Jewish than of Jewish learning. For even these tended to look for guidance to Rabbis whose mind had been moulded by the Talmud and whose outlook in consequence was anything but European, even if they were, as sometimes happened, men of very considerable general knowledge.

A revolution in this attitude towards non-Jewish learning took place in the second half of the eighteenth century among the Jews of Germany, the country which had the largest Jewish population next to Poland. The bulk of the Jews in Germany in the earlier part of the century were living in ghettos, or *Judengassen*, where cultural conditions were very similar to those among the Jews in Poland. As in Poland the language of daily intercourse was the Jewish dialect of German known as Yiddish—naturally with a smaller admixture of Polish words—and as in Poland there was great intellectual keenness which found an outlet almost exclusively in the study of Jewish learning, more attention perhaps being paid to the extra-talmudical branches. Culturally in fact the German ghettos might be regarded as a kind of annexe of Lithuanian Jewry.

German Jewry, however, possessed one feature which distinguished it sharply from Polish Jewry and endowed it with possibilities of cultural advancement. It had long been the custom of German princes to take into their service or grant special privileges to individual Jews from the ghettos who they thought might be of service to the State, especially in the sphere of finance.

Such Jews were called Hofjuden or Schutzjuden, and naturally were allowed to live outside the ghettos and to mix somewhat freely with the non-Jewish population. The Hohenzollern princes of the House of Brandenburg had been particularly liberal in pursuing this policy from the beginning of the eighteenth century, and had allowed considerable communities of such Jews to be formed in Berlin and Königsberg.

These communities, especially that of Berlin, were in some respects unique among the Jewish communities of the world.

THE ENLIGHTENMENT MOVEMENT 91

On the one hand their members, mixing with educated non-Jews, could not help realizing the value of modern European culture both in itself, as a source of intellectual improvement, and for the material benefits which it could bring in its train. On the other hand they still so to speak had one foot in the ghetto, and retained the ghetto characteristics of a firm attachment to the Jewish religion and a keen thirst for knowledge.

There was therefore among them a strong intellectual ferment which distinguished them from Jews in other countries where they were even more favourably placed materially, such as those of England, France and Holland. In the two former countries the bulk of the Jews were immersed in commercial pursuits and had little interest in culture. In Holland the Jews had a tradition of Jewish learning which they still kept up, but they no longer possessed that zest for knowledge which distinguished the German Jews.

Berlin was thus the place of all others where conditions were favourable for a commencement of the Europeanizing process among the Jews. The opportunity was not neglected, notably by one man whose example profoundly influenced the whole of Jewry. This was the celebrated Moses Mendelssohn (1729–1783), from the town of Dessau in Hanover, where his father had followed the poorly paid profession of Hebrew scribe, or copyist of scrolls of the Pentateuch and various Jewish religious documents.

Like most Jewish boys in the ghetto of any ability, he had at an early age begun to devote himself to the study of the Talmud. His teacher was David Frankel, the Rabbi of Dessau, whose favourite pupil he soon became. In 1741 Frankel was appointed Rabbi of the Berlin community, and Mendelssohn determined to follow him thither in order to continue his talmudical studies under his guidance. Against his father's will he left Dessau and made his way to Berlin. On arriving at the gate he was refused admission, as he did not possess the requisite pass. By some means, however, he obtained entry and presented himself to Frankel, who befriended him and accepted him once more as a pupil.

In Berlin the young Mendelssohn came into contact with Jews of a type which was new to him—Jews who like himself had in their early years been trained in the Talmud but who subsequently had, mainly by their own efforts, acquired some knowledge of non-Jewish subjects and had entirely discarded their prejudice against non-Jewish learning. Intercourse with them fired him with a desire to acquire similar knowledge, in the pursuit of which they willingly assisted him. Without neglecting his Hebrew studies, the young Moses studied diligently several branches of non-Jewish learning, especially Greek and Latin, and made himself a proficient German as well as Jewish scholar.

This combination of Jewish and non-Jewish learning, though rare, had by no means been unknown in the generations preceding Mendelssohn, especially in Italy, where the Jews in this respect had preserved the ancient tradition of the Judeo-Arabic period more faithfully than those of any other country. A conspicuous example was the most distinguished of them, Moses Chayim Luzzatto (1707–1747) of Padua. Luzzatto was equally at home in Italian and in Hebrew, and knew how to infuse into the latter language some of the grace of the former. He also wrote an ethical treatise, called *Mesillath Yesharim* (Path of the Upright), in which he showed himself fully alive to the value of culture and good breeding. Yet he persisted in regarding the Zohar as the source of the profoundest wisdom, and for a time, like Sabbatai Zevi, was inspired by its occultism with Messianic notions.

Another scholar of wide general culture was David Nieto of Venice (1654–1728), who in his later years became Haham (Rabbi) of the community of Spanish Jews in London, and who to a sound Rabbinic scholarship added a good knowledge of languages, mathematics, astronomy and medicine. But such scholars had almost without exception regarded their non-Jewish learning as a mere adjunct to their Jewish attainments. If they wrote at all they wrote as Jews and for or on behalf of Jews, and though they sometimes used Spanish or Italian, their chosen vehicle for literary expression was Hebrew.

Moses Mendelssohn struck out a new line. He was the first talmudically trained Jew who made the acquisition of non-Jewish culture an end in itself and gave it priority over Jewish

THE ENLIGHTENMENT MOVEMENT 93

culture. He made his watchword "enlightenment" (*Aufklärung*) in general, thus aligning himself with the most progressive non-Jewish thinkers of Germany. He devoted himself to the pursuit of truth or knowledge wherever he could find it, without any preconceived bias in favour of Jewish sources.

On the intellectual side as such he became a European pure and simple, like Spinoza before him. Unlike Spinoza, however, he continued to adhere strictly to the practice of the Jewish religion. Not only did he reject unceremoniously attempts which were made to convert him to Christianity, but he did not endeavour to alter or modify in any way traditional Jewish practice. He became, one might say, not a European, but a Europeanized Jew.

Mendelssohn had a good command of Hebrew, and wrote various works in that language, mostly on religious matters. For the most part, however, in his literary labours he sought to write as a German and for Germans. His chosen life's work was to assist his bosom friend, Gotthold Ephraim Lessing, in making German prose an elegant and precise vehicle of literary expression. As a creative writer he did not show sufficient originality to place him in the first rank of German authors. But as a critic he exercised great influence, and became one of the makers of modern German. He was the first Jew after Spinoza who made any contribution of note to European culture.

While identifying himself culturally with the German people, Mendelssohn continued to take the warmest interest in the welfare of his Jewish brethren in all parts, particularly in Germany, where he was held in very high esteem both by Jews and non-Jews. He chafed especially at the isolation of the German ghetto-Jews from the rest of the population, considering their lack of contact with the outside world to be deleterious to them both intellectually, morally and materially.

The first step necessary for overcoming this isolation was obviously that they should exchange their Yiddish dialect for the High German spoken by their surroundings. It was no easy matter, however, to induce them to make this new departure. Yiddish was associated in the Jewish mind with the study of the Talmud and the practice of Judaism; High German was associated with Christianity and free thought. To change over from Yiddish to High German was not without reason regarded by many Jews of the ghetto as the first step towards abandoning Judaism in favour of Christianity or atheism.

To overcome this prejudice, Mendelssohn published (1778–1783) a German translation of the Pentateuch which he had originally composed for the use of his own children. By this means he showed that the use of German in itself need constitute no danger to the Jewish religion. This innovation was regarded with misgiving in certain quarters where attachment to the past was particularly strong, but by most of the Jews of Germany it was warmly acclaimed as being fraught with possibilities of the highest benefit.

Outside of the ghetto—from which more and more Jews now began to emerge—this translation soon came into general use, along with that of other books of the Bible which soon followed it; and even in the ghetto it had numerous readers. Before long High German became the normal language of the Jews of Germany.

The example of Mendelssohn and his success as an author gave a tremendous impetus to the pursuit of non-Jewish knowledge by the German Jews, and by the Polish Jews who in increasing numbers began to wander into Germany at this time — some of them attracted by the fame of Mendelssohn himself. Not all of them knew how to combine this pursuit with the observance of the Jewish religion as Mendelssohn had done. Many became lax in their observance, and some even began to question whether the Mosaic law had any validity for the possessors of European enlightenment.

Mendelssohn observed this development with grave displeasure. The last thing he desired was that he should be regarded as a subverter of the Jewish religion. He took occasion to combat this tendency in the second part of his work entitled "Jerusalem," which was published in 1783, and the principal object of which was to show that the Mosaic legislation did not establish any censorship over thought, as the Christian Church (at least in Germany) sought to do. Incidentally he took occasion to address his own co-religionists, and to remind them that this legislation was still absolutely binding on them.

To make good his first point, against the Christian divines, Mendelssohn lays down that the highest activity of man consists in the pursuit of truth by the exercise of reason based on observation. Since the Bible was given to man for his benefit, its intention is not to suppress this activity, but to assist it.

There are, in Mendelssohn's view, three categories of truth. The first contains certain laws of thought and axiomatic propositions such as those of logic and mathematics. The second contains the general theories of material and moral science, and the laws of nature established by observation and reasoning. The third contains casual and accidental happenings, subject to no rule but worthy of note, like the facts of history. The Bible has nothing to do with the first kind of truth, which is discoverable by the reason without the aid of revelation. But it is invaluable if not indispensable for the discovery of certain truths of the second kind, such as those relating to the nature of God and the moral welfare of man; and it also contains many of the third kind.

In his ardour for enlightenment Mendelssohn seems not to have noticed that his basic proposition, that the felicity of man lies in the pursuit of knowledge by the exercise of his reason, was much more a Hellenic than a Hebraic idea. To the Rabbis of the Talmud and Midrash goodness or righteousness was more important than truth, and knowledge was valuable only in so far as it led to righteousness. And even the Jewish philosophers of the Middle Ages, who cultivated every branch of knowledge known in their time, would probably have demurred to it; for to them the knowledge of God was not merely one kind of knowledge among others, as to Mendelssohn, but the supreme kind, to which all others were subsidiary.

By his theory of truth Mendelssohn was in fact introducing a far-reaching innovation into the Jewish religion, one which had a most important bearing on the nature of Jewish study. Though he found an honoured place in his scheme for the Bible, he said nothing of the Talmud, and it is difficult to see what value he could have assigned to it as a source of truth. Elsewhere in his writings he does actually speak somewhat disparagingly of the Talmud, as of something which had little interest for the modern Jew. He was therefore as far removed from the *talmide chakhamim* of Lithuania as were the Chassidim of southern Poland, but in the opposite direction. For them the Talmud was too intellectual, for him it was not intellectual enough; they attacked it in the name of emotionalism, he in the name of a superior form of reasoning.

Yet while thus relegating to the background the study of the Talmud, Mendelssohn continued to maintain that the Jewish people had received from God through the hand of Moses a legislation which was still binding on them. In a later passage of his "Jerusalem" he suddenly, in a kind of afterthought, adjures his fellow-Jews to remain true to the religion of their ancestors. The laws of the Jewish religion, he affirms, embody the will of God, which must be obeyed. "I do not see," he says, "how those who have been born in the House of Israel can in any conscientious manner disburden themselves of the law. It is permitted to us to reflect on the law, to probe into its spirit, here and there where the lawgiver has given no reason to surmise a reason ... But so long as we can point to no release from the law as authentic as its imposition, our ratiocination cannot free us from the obedience which we owe to the law, and respect for God draws a line between thought and conduct which no man of conscience would dare to overstep."

Mendelssohn nowhere specifies what exactly he meant by the Mosaic law, but to judge by his actions we must suppose that he had in mind the code of the Shulchan Arukh which had for nearly two centuries been the accepted rule of Jewish conduct.

Thus Mendelssohn introduced no change in the Jewish religion, in spite of his Hellenic theories of truth and knowledge. He was like a man who finds himself along with others locked in a room and who succeeds in unlocking the door but refuses to go out, and pleads earnestly with the others to do the same.

Nor was his plea ineffective. A great many of the "enlightened" Jews, it is true, went over to Christianity in the years immediately after Mendelssohn's death. But the majority followed in his footsteps. They became "new-fashioned" in their speech and garb and many details of their conduct. They did not keep the minutiæ of the Jewish law with the same strictness as the "old-fashioned," and they made their synagogue service more decorous. But the chief difference between them was that the latter continued to study the Talmud and very little else, while the former studied anything but the Talmud. It was the difference between a plant left in its own soil and one transplanted to another soil in which its chances of survival are problematical.

The new attitude of the "enlightened" Jews towards the Talmud brought with it as an inevitable corollary a complete recasting of the Jewish system of education. In the Jewish schools of the ghetto the curriculum up to this time had been much the same as in those of Poland. In the elementary school the child was taught to read Hebrew, to say his prayers, to translate the Pentateuch, and perhaps some other parts of the Bible (in northern Europe into Yiddish), and generally to conduct himself as a Jew. A little instruction in arithmetic and general subjects might be added, but was usually not; the child was left to pick up these as best he could. If he showed promise he was pushed on at the earliest possible age to the study of the Talmud, to which thenceforth his attention was mainly if not exclusively directed. The Talmud thus constituted the one indispensable element in the higher education of the Jew; the whole of the elementary curriculum was framed with an eye to its eventual study, and from it all other advanced studies branched out.

That this system of education was utterly unsuitable for the modern generation of the Jews of Germany was self-evident. The problem for the "enlightened" German Jews was to substitute for it a system which should enable the Jewish boy to acquire a sound knowledge of modern subjects without weakening his attachment to his ancestral religion.

Special attention was devoted to this problem by David Friedländer (1750–1834), the son-in-law of the wealthy Berlin banker Daniel Itzig (1723–1799), and a great friend and admirer of Mendelssohn. Without being highly gifted intellectually, Friedländer was well versed both in Jewish and non-Jewish subjects—he wrote in Hebrew a commentary on the "Ethics of the Fathers" and lectured on philosophy in the University of Königsberg, besides writing many works in German; when

Mendelssohn died he aspired to take his place as the intellectual leader of German Jewry.

In 1781 Friedländer in conjunction with his father-in-law, Itzig, had founded a school for Jewish youth in which the chief subjects of the curriculum were non-Jewish, but in which considerable time was also devoted to Hebrew, Bible and Talmud. This school for some time set the norm for Jewish education in Germany outside the ghetto, though the tendency was always for the non-Jewish subjects to encroach on the Jewish. The Jewish training given in such schools was sufficient to enable the pupil to carry out correctly the precepts of his religion, and to make him feel that he was a Jew. It might also in some cases give him a tincture of Jewish culture, but not more than a tincture; more frequently it would leave him ignorant that there was such a thing.

In the ghetto also the old order did not remain entirely unchanged, though naturally it did not undergo the same drastic alteration as outside. The first impulse came from a purely external source. In 1781 the Emperor Joseph II of Austria, in an access of liberalism rather in advance of his time, issued his so-called *Toleranzedict*, which removed many of the disabilities of the Jews of his dominions and ordered them somewhat peremptorily to teach non-Jewish subjects in their schools, and through the medium of High German, so as to fit the pupils to take a more active part in the life of the State.

To most of the Rabbis of Austria and Germany this order was far from welcome, as they scented in it a danger to the study of the Talmud. It found, however, an unexpected champion in the person of Naphthali Hirsch Wessely, the close friend and collaborator of Mendelssohn. In April, 1782, Wessely sent a circular letter in Hebrew, entitled "Words of Peace and Truth," to all the leading Rabbis of Austria enthusiastically welcoming the Kaiser's rescript and urging them to give effect to it by all the means in their power. He also drew up a curriculum which he recommended them for use in their schools, and in which he included, along with the Talmud, such subjects as natural science and astronomy—for these also, in his opinion, were necessary for a proper understanding of the Bible.

In Rabbinic circles Wessely enjoyed high esteem as a learned and pious Jew. Most of the Rabbis of Austria and Germany, however, found his educational proposals far too radical—besides being somewhat unpractical—and many even of his best friends condemned them unreservedly, while none ventured to espouse them openly. In Italy, however, where the Jews had never been prejudiced against non-Jewish studies like those of Germany, they had a more favourable reception.

Nothing daunted, therefore, Wessely now addressed himself to the community of Trieste where the population was Italian though under Austrian rule. Here his ideas were taken up with enthusiasm, and before long schools more or less on the lines which he indicated were opened in Trieste and other places. The example of the Italian Rabbis was not without its effect on those of Germany and Austria. Gradually all but the most fanatical opened their eyes to the necessity of allowing the Jewish youth to obtain at least the rudiments of a non-Jewish education, even at the risk that they might thereby be seduced from the study of the Talmud.

CHAPTER IX

THE HASKALAH MOVEMENT

IN devoting himself to the pursuit of enlightenment, Mendelssohn had adopted the natural course of making German his usual vehicle of literary expression. He continued, like the *talmide chakhamim*, to regard Hebrew as a more or less sacred language, the proper use of which was in discussing subjects connected with the *torah*. He still used Hebrew when writing in a religious vein, as for a commentary on a biblical book. But when dealing with non-religious topics, he used German, even when addressing himself specifically to his fellow-Jews, as when he discussed the relations of Jews with non-Jews.

In this respect his example was not followed by some of his most ardent admirers and disciples. These towards the end of his life included a number of young men either from the German ghettos or from Poland, who like himself had been brought up in the study of the Talmud and, as a kind of by-product of that study, had learnt to write Hebrew fluently, and who after completing their talmudic studies applied themselves to the acquisition of modern knowledge. Whether, however, because their talmudic training was more thorough than his or because their German training was less thorough, they retained to a much greater degree their affection for Hebrew, and continued to find it more natural to express themselves in that language than in German, even on subjects which had no connection with Judaism and for dealing with which a Hebrew vocabulary had still to be created.

This predilection for Hebrew was shared by them with an older man who stood more on a level with Mendelssohn and was regarded by the younger generation with hardly less esteem. This was Naphthali Hirsch (Hartwig) Wessely (1725–1805), already mentioned above as an educational reformer.

THE HASKALAH MOVEMENT 101

Wessely, who came of Polish stock, was born in Altona and received in his youth a good training in Talmud. One of his teachers, however, a Polish Jew named Solomon Hanau, inspired him with a strong attachment for the Bible and its language, and though he subsequently acquired a good secular training, Hebrew philology and composition remained his ruling passion throughout his life. In 1774 he came to Berlin and formed there a close friendship with Mendelssohn, whose efforts to enlighten his co-religionists he zealously seconded. He was especially interested in the Hebraic side of Mendelssohn's work, and became the moving spirit in bringing to completion the Hebrew commentary which Mendelssohn had planned to accompany his translation of the Pentateuch.

This commentary was designed by Mendelssohn to show readers of Hebrew that his German translation could be used without any detriment to the cause of the Jewish religion. It was commenced by a Polish Jew of considerable talmudic learning named Solomon Dubno, who wrote the commentary on Genesis. Dubno then had qualms about continuing the work, and Mendelssohn himself wrote the commentary to Exodus. Finding the work, however, not too congenial, he handed it over to Wessely and some of the younger Hebraists, and they produced a commentary on the whole of the Hebrew Scriptures which was issued under the title of *biur* (lit. "explanation").

The characteristic of the *biur* was that, while retaining the traditional view of the inspiration of the Bible, it rejected all far-fetched interpretations of the text and sought to explain it strictly according to the rules of grammar and philology.

The *biur* immediately became popular with the Hebrew-reading public of Germany, and it was soon followed by a much bolder venture in modernism. In Königsberg—which for the Jews of Germany was a kind of outpost of Berlin—two young Hebrew teachers named Isaac Euchel and Mendel Bresselau conceived the idea of founding a Hebrew magazine which should deal with literary and current topics on the lines of the German magazines then in vogue. Wessely gave them his warm support and Mendelssohn his blessing, and in 1783 they issued in Berlin the first number of a Hebrew magazine called

Meassef ("Gleaner"). It made on the whole a favourable impression, and continued to appear more or less regularly for the next twenty years, sometimes in Berlin and sometimes in other places.

The *Meassef* never possessed any great literary merit, and it made no original contribution either to German or to Jewish culture. Its chief function was to stimulate in its readers an interest in modern European culture. In doing so it dug its own grave, for it was this very interest in European culture which caused the Hebrew language to be neglected by the German Jews of the next generation. Its chief importance therefore may be considered to lie in the fact that it constituted the bridge by which the "enlightenment" movement was conveyed from the Jews of Germany to those of Poland, to whom otherwise it might never have penetrated.

There were a number of reasons why the Jews of Poland (which in connection with the Jews of this time must be taken to mean the pre-partition Poland, including Galicia, Posen, Lithuania and much of the Ukraine) should have been more impervious to the Mendelssohnian influence than those of Germany. The study of the Talmud was more strongly entrenched there than in the ghettos of Germany; the learned Talmudists were even more numerous, enjoyed even greater respect and wielded even greater authority. Again, in Germany, the Jews could not but be conscious that the Yiddish dialect of German which they spoke was a mere jargon when compared with the High German spoken by educated non-Jews; but in Poland the Jews, who spoke the same jargon, and in a more debased form, were not conscious of any inferiority in it to Lithuanian, or even Polish.

In any case it was in their opinion the one language through which the Talmud could be taught, and this was sufficient to make it precious in their eyes. Finally, facilities for non-Jewish study were in Poland almost non-existent for Jews, if not also for non-Jews; Poland was practically cut off from the West, especially after it came under the rule of the barbarous Russians.

Hence if all the Jewish writers of Germany had followed Mendelssohn's example in using German as the language of "enlightenment," it is difficult to see how the Jews of Poland could as a body have become interested in that movement. Individuals who thirsted for modern knowledge would as before have continued to emigrate to Germany and would there have become German-speaking and German-writing; and their work would have remained unknown to their brethren across the border. But the *Meassef* could be read and appreciated by the Jews of Poland; it could at least awaken in them the thirst for enlightenment and suggest to them ways of satisfying it without Germanizing themselves.

The effects of the new spirit first showed themselves in Galicia, which came under Austrian rule, and where consequently it was much easier for the Jews to acquire secular knowledge than in the parts of Poland annexed to Russia. At the beginning of the nineteenth century talmudic students there began in increasing numbers to study non-Jewish subjects and to pay particular attention to the philology of the Hebrew language. They received the name of *maskilim* (singular, *maskil*, lit. "intellectual," hence "rationalist"), and their movement was known as *haskalah* (rationalism).

The *maskilim* were distinguished from the ordinary talmudical students not only by the wider range of their knowledge, but also by the critical and often hostile spirit with which they regarded both the Talmud and traditional Jewish practice. For the Bible on the other hand they retained the utmost veneration, not, however, so much on account of its contents as because it was the pure and original fountain of the Hebrew language. Their advanced views naturally brought them into sharp conflict with the Chassidim, who were very numerous and influential in Galicia, and the more bigoted of whom considered the name *maskil* as synonymous with freethinker or atheist.

The *haskalah* was for the Jews of Poland what *Aufklärung* was for the Jews of Germany. It provided them with a form of culture alternative to that of the Talmud, but one that was still Jewish. Although the *maskilim* were attracted to the Bible primarily for linguistic reasons, they could not easily separate the language from the contents, and were bound to be much more profoundly affected by the spirit of the Bible than those who read it in a German translation, or who had to translate it into German in order to understand it. Nor could the *maskilim* regard the Talmud with the same indifference as the *Aufgeklärten*. Certainly the Hebrew of the Talmud was from a literary point of view far inferior to that of the Bible. Nevertheless it was still Hebrew, and some knowledge of it was indispensable to the would-be Hebrew writer. Hence an acquaintance with the Talmud formed an integral part of the *haskalah*, which was thus much nearer to the Talmudic culture than the German *Aufklärung*.

The *haskalah* movement in Galicia in the early part of the nineteenth century was represented by some brilliant writers who made notable contributions to Hebrew literature. They were unable, however, to exercise much influence on the mass of the population. Chassidic obscurantism was too strongly entrenched for them to overthrow. In spite of all their appeals the religious authorities stubbornly refused to implement the ordinance of Joseph II, and preserved the old system of Jewish education with little if any change. In Galicia the *haskalah* failed to affect the life of the mass of the Jews to any appreciable extent. From Galicia, however, it spread to Poland proper and Lithuania, and here its effects were far more marked, especially at first in the educational field.

At the end of the eighteenth century there were not wanting Jews in Poland who felt that the whole Jewish educational system there was too narrow, and that the inclusion in it of some non-Jewish subjects was urgently required. This idea was countenanced by no less an authority than the celebrated talmudic scholar Elijah of Wilna, who was held in as great esteem by the Jews of Poland as Mendelssohn by the Jews of Germany.

Elijah had spent his whole life in the study of Jewish literature, especially the Talmud. Yet in his old age he urged one of his disciples to translate into Hebrew the Geometry of Euclid, while another at his suggestion wrote in Hebrew a book explaining the scientific principles of some simple inventions.

At the end of the eighteenth century, however, Jewish public opinion in Poland was still far from ripe for any change in the existing educational system. In Germany the whole outlook of the Jews in educational matters had been altered by their adoption of High German instead of Yiddish as their ordinary language of intercourse. This substitution had commenced with the use of High German for translating the Bible, and was hardly possible for the Jews of Poland. The substitution of Polish was equally out of the question—if indeed it would have had any educational value. If the requisite public opinion was to be created in Poland, it would have to be through a propaganda in the Hebrew language; and of this, seeing that Hebrew itself was learnt there as an adjunct of the study of the Talmud, there was little prospect.

At length, however, the spread of the *haskalah* from Galicia produced the man who was able to solve the problem. This was a Jew from Kremenitz in Volhynia, named Isaac Baer Levinsohn (1788–1860). In his early years Levinsohn acquired a good knowledge of the Talmud, and later he came into contact with the leading Galician *maskilim*. With his mind broadened by such intercourse, he made it his object to break down the crass prejudices which Polish Jewry had imbibed not only against non-Jewish learning, but also against all Jewish learning outside of the Talmud and the Pentateuch.

For this purpose he published in 1828 a book in Hebrew entitled *Te'udah be-Yisroel* (An Appeal to Israel) in which he considered the question, "what learning, apart from the Talmud and its commentaries, was necessary for a Jew to acquire for the perfection and refinement of his nature as a man and a Jew." He derived the answer from Hebrew literature itself. "He sought out and found in the Talmud and the Midrashim, and in medieval Hebrew literature, numerous sayings and expressions which made it perfectly obvious that knowledge of foreign languages and general subjects of learning (and still more a knowledge of Hebrew and its grammar and literature), so far from being regarded as a sin, was actually a sacred obligation laid on every Jew who wished to understand the nature of his religion and faith and to be convinced of the genuineness of its foundation.

"He showed that the very Sages of the Talmud itself knew foreign languages and various sciences, and learned much from Greek and Roman writers, and that husbandry and manual labour were frequently commended in the Talmud and later literature; while as for handicrafts, many of the Sages of the Talmud were themselves craftsmen and artisans."[1] The lesson of *Te'udah be-Yisroel* was driven home by Levinsohn in a second work, *Beth Yehudah* (House of Judah), published in 1838, in which he elaborated a plan for reorganizing Jewish education in Russia, with Rabbinical seminaries, elementary Jewish schools throughout Poland, and agricultural and industrial schools.

Levinsohn wrote in an easy and attractive Hebrew style, and his works exercised a considerable influence on Russian Jewry. He was often called by his admirers the Russian Mendelssohn, and certainly like Mendelssohn he sought to make non-Jewish studies an integral part of Jewish education. But it was only in the sphere of elementary education that they pursued the same path; in that of higher education they diverged. Mendelssohn left practically no place for the Talmud in the higher education of the German Jews; Levinsohn on the other hand still regarded it as an essential part, perhaps the principal part, of the higher education of the Russian Jew. The consequence was that while in Germany Hebrew was largely forgotten by the modernized Jews, in Russia there grew up a large public which perused with avidity the new *haskalah* literature, written in Hebrew but with a modern outlook.

In Russia, as in Galicia, there was considerable friction between the *maskilim* and the orthodox, who, though less bigoted than the Chassidim, continued to nourish strong prejudices against modern education. These prejudices were for a time accentuated by the efforts of the Russian Government to disseminate such education amongst them. In 1842 the Russian Minister of Education commissioned a German Jew, Max Lilienthal, who had been appointed Rabbi at Riga, to discuss with the orthodox Rabbis of Russia a plan for establishing Jewish modern schools under Government auspices. The Rabbis—not without reason—suspected the Government of a design to win the Jewish children over to Christianity, and the only effect of the discussions was to

[1] Klausner, *History of Modern Hebrew Literature*, Chapter II.

harden them in their attachment to the old-fashioned methods of education.

Both enlightenment and *haskalah* in their more advanced forms brought to the notice of the Jews ideas and theories which seemed to conflict with Jewish religious teaching, in fact, with all religious doctrine. The high priest of enlightenment was the free-thinker Voltaire, and its text-book the sceptical Encyclopédie of Diderot and D'Alembert. How was the Jew to deal with the anti-religious arguments adduced by these and similar writers? Was he to ignore them or to try to refute them? And if he could not refute them, what was to be the effect on his religious belief and practices?

A similar problem had faced the Jews of the Moslem world when in the early Middle Ages they became acquainted through Arabic translations with the works of the neo-Platonists and Aristotle. In their endeavours to solve it they had produced the so-called Jewish religious philosophy of the Middle Ages (*vide supra*, Chapter v). This could, and did, still satisfy the religious doubts and questionings of those Jews for whom Spinoza and Voltaire were non-existent—and these still formed the great majority, even among scholars. But for the growing number who were acquainted with modern thought it was not sufficient. Religion was now exposed to objections to which an answer could not be found in the old philosophy. Reason spoke now in a voice somewhat different from that which it had used six or seven centuries previously; and if religion was to be harmonized with it, a new philosophy was required.

The most important contribution to the solution of this problem, and one which greatly influenced subsequent Jewish thought, was made by a *maskil* named Nachman Krochmal (1785–1849), of Brody in Galicia. Krochmal was given by his father access to modern books, from which he obtained an excellent knowledge of history and philosophy. These studies led him to investigate deeply the problem of the survival of the Jewish people—how it had survived in the past and how it was to survive in the future. He saw the great danger to Jewish survival in the future in the divorce between faith and reason. Faith was strong in the Chassidim, but it was based among them on utterly irrational assumptions; on the other hand the rational outlook of the *maskilim* tended to undermine their faith. If the Jewish people was to survive, it could not dispense either with faith or with rationalism.

The Jewish philosophers of the Middle Ages had also recognized the vital importance of combining faith with reason, but it was in order to preserve not the Jewish people but the Jewish religion. Krochmal showed his modernity by making the people the centre of interest, and treating the religion as, so to speak, a function of the people. He was correspondingly modern in his approach to the problem. In his magnum opus—which he himself called *Gates of Purified Faith*, but which was edited after his death by his friend Leopold Zunz under the title of *Guide to the Perplexed of the Age*, he focuses attention on the question: what is it that has enabled the Jewish people to survive up to the present, and outlive so many other peoples which were more powerful in their day?

To this question he gives an answer at once religious and philosophical. Every nation, he says, depends for its existence on the activity of a certain spirit which endows it with creative activity of a particular kind. Thus the spirit of the Greek people rendered it creative in the field of art and speculation, the spirit of the Roman people rendered it creative in the field of administration and military organization. Now in respect of this spirit every nation goes through three stages. In the first the spirit is formative, and gives to the nation its peculiar character; in the second it is preservative, and enables the nation to develop and perfect the productions of the first period; in the third it falls into decay, and finally disappears, along with the nation.

The Jewish people has also gone through these three stages more than once, yet has not disappeared. The reason is this. The spirit of every other nation has some material attachment which makes it finite and destructible. But the spirit of the Jewish people is purely spiritual, and therefore, though it is subject to decay, it possesses the power of regenerating itself and the Jewish people along with it.

It cannot be said that with this theory Krochmal solved the problem of combining faith with rationalism. The question still remained, in what was Jewish spirituality to consist in the modern world. To this question one does not find that Krochmal provided an answer. But at any rate he narrowed the field of inquiry and pointed out where exactly attention should be concentrated. He indicated the possibility of finding the basis for a renewed faith in "Jewish tradition," a term to which he gave a new significance as something akin to revelation, yet broader and more flexible. In this way he saved many from being swept away by the current of unbelief, even if he could not restore to them a living faith.

Another Hebrew writer who similarly sought to combat the spread of irreligion among his fellow *maskilim* was Samuel David Luzzatto (1800-1865) of Trieste, a member of the same family as the Moses Chayim Luzzatto mentioned above (p. 92). An accomplished linguist and talmudical scholar, in 1829 he was appointed professor of Bible, Jewish History and Theology at the Rabbinical Seminary which had just been opened at Padua.

Luzzatto had an aversion to metaphysics, but he was keenly interested in ethics, especially Jewish ethics. He observed with deep concern the harmful influence exercised by the *haskalah* on many of the younger Jews in making them indifferent not only to the beliefs and ceremonies of the Jewish religion, but also to its ethical precepts. In his correspondence he returns repeatedly to this subject, and while calling attention to the evil suggests a remedy in the shape of a new notion of the place of Jewish ethics in modern life. He saw in the Jewish people the great upholders of the spirit of religion as opposed to that of rationalism. The search for knowledge and truth by means of rational investigation he called "Atticism," and he did not question its value, for Jews as well as for non-Jews.

But the Jews were the descendants of Abraham who "kept the way of the Lord to practise righteousness and judgment,"[1] and as such they were the heirs of a striving—called by him "Abrahamism"—the object of which was to establish a personal relation between man and God and to keep alive the spirit of faith in the world. The two foundations of Abrahamism were belief in divine recompense and retribution, and the virtue of

[1] Gen. xviii, 19.

kindheartedness or compassion, which was alien to the spirit of Hellenism but in regard to which the Talmud declared: "He who has no pity is not of the seed of Abraham." These qualities were to be learnt partly from the Bible, but still more from the talmudic literature, which therefore should still be made the basis of Jewish conduct.

CHAPTER X

EMANCIPATION AND JEWISH LAW

THE movement of European thought in the eighteenth century influenced the Jews of Western Europe no less on its political than on its cultural side. At the same time that it aroused their interest in the problem of enlightenment and of secular education generally, it also forced on their attention a political question with a similar profound if indirect bearing on their religious future. The enlightened public opinion of Europe demanded, in the name of the "Rights of Man," that the Jews should be freed from the civil and political disabilities under which they laboured, and admitted to equality of rights with the rest of the citizens.

Jewish opinion itself was divided on the subject. Those who favoured enlightenment were also anxious for political emancipation and equality of rights; when Mendelssohn urged his fellow-Jews to discard Yiddish for German as their ordinary language and to familiarize themselves with modern culture, one of his avowed objects was to qualify them for the grant of citizenship which he hoped would soon be conferred on them. Others again, with whom the religious interest was paramount, could not help feeling that emancipation would place new temptations in the way of the Jews and perhaps weaken their allegiance to Jewish law; and they therefore looked on it with indifference if not hostility.

The first country to confer full civic rights on its Jewish subjects was the United States, soon after the Declaration of Independence. The Jews here, being of a type which was more influenced by worldly than by religious considerations, naturally accepted the grant without misgivings. In France, however, when the question of emancipating the Jews was taken in hand soon after the Revolution of 1789, a cleavage in

Jewish opinion soon made itself apparent. The leading Jew of Alsace at that time was Berr Isaac Berr, a man of progressive outlook, but at the same time strongly attached to the traditional form of Judaism. Berr was well aware of the urgent need of his fellow-Jews of Alsace for full civil rights, but he was equally aware of the need of Rabbinic authority for their moral welfare.

He tried to combine the two things by drawing up, in 1792, a petition to the National Assembly—of which he had been elected a member—demanding equal rights for the Jews of France, and at the same time requesting that the autonomy and authority of the Rabbis for the internal affairs of the Jewish communities should be recognized and maintained. Other Jewish deputies, however, objected to the request; and in deference to them Berr did not press it. There could be no doubt, however, that in this matter he spoke for a large body of Jews in all Western countries.

Shortly afterwards full civil rights were granted to the French Jews, including those of Alsace. The grant was naturally not received by all sections in the same spirit. The Jews of Paris and of Bordeaux, who were French-speaking and had mixed freely with non-Jews, welcomed it enthusiastically, and they showed no scruple in disregarding the obligations of Jewish law when they conflicted with their duties as French citizens, especially in the matter of military service.

Considerably different was the reaction of the Jews of Alsace. These were rooted in the German ghetto, and still largely spoke Yiddish. They had a deep respect for the Talmud and the Rabbis who expounded it, and looked with some disdain on non-Jews. Whatever value they may have attached to their new status, they were not willing that it should in any way interfere with their Jewish way of life. In all the countries over which Napoleon extended his empire the Jews automatically received the same civil rights as the rest of the population; and in all the same distinction appeared among them as in France.

The differences between the two sections were brought into relief, and to some extent reconciled, by the Council of Jewish Notables which met in Paris in 1806. This Council, consisting of about a hundred members thoroughly representative of the Jewish communities of the French Empire, was convened by Napoleon in order to provide him with assurances that profession of the Jewish religion was really compatible with French citizenship. For this purpose he set before them twelve questions, on their answer to which his decision would depend. From an early point the discussions on these questions—all of which were ultimately answered to the Emperor's satisfaction —revealed the existence in the Council of two sections, a progressive and a conservative.

The leader of the former section was Abraham Furtado, a merchant of Bordeaux whose ancestors had until recently been Marranos (crypto-Jews) in Portugal. Like most Jews of Marrano stock, Furtado was much more strongly attached to the monotheistic creed and the ethics of Judaism than to the talmudic law. The leader of the Conservative section was David Sinzheim, a patriarchal Rabbi from Strasburg, a man of deep piety and great talmudical learning, a close friend of Berr Isaac Berr and like him commendably free from bigotry.

In spite of the differences in outlook between the two sections, they found no difficulty in coming to an agreement over every question set by the Emperor except one. This was, whether mixed marriages between Jews and non-Jews could be permitted by Jewish law. On this question a heated controversy arose between the two sections. It was obvious that an affirmative answer would open the way to an eventual absorption of the Jews in their non-Jewish surroundings. Nevertheless Furtado could see no harm in following the Emperor's suggestion, while to Sinzheim it was of course utterly unacceptable. Eventually a compromise was reached, and an answer was submitted stating that the Rabbis could not be expected themselves to celebrate marriages between Jews and non-Jews, but that they would continue to regard as Jews and Jewesses those who had contracted such marriages.

A religious problem of equal importance was raised by another of the Emperor's questions. This was, whether French Jews were prepared to recognize France as their fatherland, the French as their brethren, and the law of the state as binding on them also. An affirmative answer to this question might be regarded as a renunciation of Jewish hopes for a national restoration. It might also be taken to imply that the Jews would cease to regard the precepts of their own law as more binding on them than those of the civil law, a change which conceivably might gravely affect their attitude towards their Rabbis and to the observance of their religion.

Considering that fourteen years before Berr Isaac Berr had sought to provide against this very danger in the petition which he had drafted for the National Assembly (*vide supra*), it might have been expected that this question would provoke a storm of controversy. Actually, however, it received an affirmative answer unanimously and with acclamation. Probably in the excitement of the moment men like Berr and Sinzheim were swept off their feet and did not notice its subtle but far-reaching implications in the sphere of religion.

In order to lend more weight to the answers given by the notables to his questions, Napoleon in the next year convoked what he called a Jewish Sanhedrin—consisting largely of the same members as the conference of notables but with a larger proportion of Rabbis—which he called upon to ratify them. Before this assembly Furtado laid a resolution declaring that Judaism consisted of two distinct elements, one purely religious and the other political and juridical, and that while the former was unalterable the latter had lost its validity since the downfall of the Jewish state. This was accepted by the Sanhedrin without demur.

To Furtado and those who shared his views this declaration can only have meant that in the arranging of their lives the claims of French citizenship were to take precedence over those of Jewish law. They were henceforth not Jews domiciled in France but French citizens of the Jewish faith, or Frenchmen of the Jewish persuasion. This faith or persuasion might for the time being remain the same in all particulars as the religion of their fathers. But it no longer drew sustenance from one of the chief roots of that religion, namely, the authority of the Rabbi. For in the eyes of the old-fashioned Jew the Rabbi still possessed an authority derived, if only in the imagination of his followers, from that very juridical element in the Jewish religion which the Sanhedrin had discarded as invalid.

The new type of Jew might still respect the person of the Rabbi and follow his teaching, but they could not acknowledge his authority. And similarly with the Messianic hope which, as realists, they practically renounced; even to the old-fashioned Jews it might be no more than a dream, but it was a dream that haunted them and would not let them stray far from the law of Moses. In turning their minds from this dream the "Frenchmen—or others—of the Jewish persuasion"—were bound to become more critical of their traditional religion and to chafe more at its restrictions.

As if to remove from the Jewish law any suspicion of juridical authority, Napoleon shortly afterwards made the French Rabbinate a state service, bringing it into line with the Christian clergy, which he had already treated in the same way. The new Government Rabbis naturally in many instances showed themselves more eager to make of their flock good Frenchmen than good Jews. With their connivance the French Jews—except in Alsace—entered with zest on the path of what was called "assimilation"—that is, attempting to identify themselves with their non-Jewish surroundings not only politically but also socially; and before long they became notorious for their laxity in Jewish religious observance.

A few years after Napoleon's institution of a state Rabbinate the Czar of Russia imposed the same system on the unemancipated Jews of that country; and it is interesting to compare their reaction to the innovation with that of the French Jews. In France Napoleon had no difficulty in finding suitable candidates for his government posts, and the Rabbis he appointed were accepted by the communities without demur and as a matter of course. In Russia no Rabbis of standing would consent to hold office as Government servants, and those Rabbis who did so were boycotted by the communities, though these were taxed for their upkeep.

It may well be surmised, however, that in the Sanhedrin itself there were not a few who did not take the declaration of that body altogether at its face value, and who interpreted it in a manner which involved little or no sacrifice of their

Jewish identity. Certain it is that for more than one generation a large number—perhaps the majority—of Jews in Western Europe showed no anxiety to become "citizens of the Jewish persuasion," and even when they acquired civil rights continued to regard Jewish law as no less binding than the law of the land, and to respect the authority of their Rabbis.

Thus in England the spiritual head of the Ashkenazic (German-descended) Jewish community from 1802 to 1842 was Solomon Herschell, a Rabbi distinctly of the ghetto type, and his successor, Marcus Nathan Adler—who was for many years Chief Rabbi of nearly all the Jewish communities of England—while a man of wide general culture, was far from being an "Englishman of the Jewish persuasion," and exercised a real Rabbinic authority. And there must have been many Jews ready to echo the criticism of emancipation made as late as 1840 by the noted Italian Jewish scholar, Samuel David Luzzatto: "The fortunes of our people do not depend on emancipation, but on our love of one another and on our being united with ties of brotherhood like children of one family. That is our fortune, which is diminishing and being lost in the shadow of emancipation."

CHAPTER XI

THE EARLY REFORM MOVEMENT AND THE CONSERVATIVE REACTION

EMANCIPATION in France, as we have seen, produced almost immediately two effects of note in the religious life of the French Jews. One was that the ordinary layman tended to become much more lax in his observance of the ceremonial law. The other—in some way the obverse of this one—was that the French Rabbi ceased to be a Rabbi in the old sense—that is, a man whose word within certain spheres was law—and became merely a preacher or clergyman who could at most exercise moral suasion. Officially, however, the religion remained unchanged. No alterations, beyond a few æsthetic improvements, were made in the form of service, and no part of Jewish law or belief was formally abrogated. The result was that the French Jew continued to profess a religion which in many cases he no longer pretended to practise.

In Germany the official religion did not escape so lightly, for two reasons. For one thing, the struggle for emancipation was much harder for the Jews of Germany than for those of France. The leaders in that struggle found that in order to obtain civic rights something more was required of them than to subscribe to the decisions of the Paris Sanhedrin, and they considered the prize worth the sacrifice.

Then again the Jews of Germany took their religion more seriously than those of France. They were not content to profess one thing and practise another, but when they found that the obligations of citizenship conflicted with those of Judaism, they revised their Judaism in order to bring it into harmony with the new conditions.

The prime mover in this development was Israel Jacobsohn

(1769–1828), a wealthy Jew of Westphalia, who, although a business man, was not without a knowledge both of the Talmud and of non-Jewish subjects and possessed considerable oratorical ability. Jacobsohn early threw himself into the struggle for the removal of Jewish civic disabilities, and became the acknowledged leader of the Jews of western Germany. He saw his efforts in this field crowned with success when in 1808 King Jerome, Napoleon's nominee on the throne of Westphalia, conferred full civil rights on the Jews of western Germany, naturally on the conditions laid down by the Paris Sanhedrin. Jacobsohn accepted the gift with alacrity, and took a leading part in organizing the Rabbinate of Westphalia on the lines instituted in France.

Jacobsohn was often called the German Furtado, but unlike Furtado and the French Jews he did not stop at this point. He was not satisfied that the Jew should know himself to be a German citizen in his ordinary daily life—he wished him to be constantly reminded of the fact even in the synagogue.

For this purpose he built at his own expense a small synagogue—which he called a temple—at Seesen, in Hanover, in which he arranged the service according to his own ideas. A German sermon was made an integral part of the service—a great innovation in Germany, though sermons in Italian or Spanish had always formed part of the service elsewhere. German prayers and hymns were introduced into the liturgy alongside of the established Hebrew ones, and all mention of a messianic redemption of the Jewish people was omitted. The chanting was accompanied by an organ, and a confirmation service for boys and girls was instituted.

Jacobsohn's reforms met a need of the time. There were now many Jews in Germany possessed of a German education and regarding themselves as German citizens to whom the old-fashioned Jewish synagogue service with its lack of grace and dignity was utterly distasteful, but who could see no alternative except in the church, which was even more distasteful. They found in Jacobsohn's temple more or less what they wanted, and consequently before long it had many imitators.

In 1818 a Reform-Tempel-Verein was formed in Hamburg, and under its auspices an imposing synagogue was built, and a gifted preacher engaged in the person of Gotthold Salomon, who made the sermon a power in the Jewish community. The new "Reform" movement, as it was called, was denounced by a number of Rabbis of the orthodox school as being in contravention of Jewish law, but its adherents also found certain Rabbis who gave it their sanction.

It had been the fond hope of Jacobsohn that his reforms would break down the anti-Jewish prejudice of the Christian population in Germany and render the emancipation of the Jews secure. This hope was not fulfilled. As soon as the French were driven out of Western Germany anti-Jewish prejudice revived there in full force, and the Jews were deprived of many of the privileges conferred on them by the French rulers. Many Jews in order to obtain a place in the Government service embraced Christianity. It was obvious that if Jacobsohn's objects were to be achieved, something more drastic was required than a mere reform of the synagogue service. In the generous but mistaken notion that German Jew-hatred was due to defects of the Jews, three young men in Berlin, Leopold Zunz, Eduard Gans, and Moses Moser—all destined to achieve distinction later in various branches—formed in November, 1819, a "Society for spreading Culture and Knowledge among the Jews" (Verein für Cultur und Wissenschaft der Juden), the object of which was to make the Jews more worthy of the esteem of their fellow-Germans. The society was soon joined by David Friedländer and Israel Jacobsohn, and a little later by Heinrich Heine, and it managed to enrol about fifty members in Berlin and twenty in Hamburg.

Those who joined were required to take an oath that they would not become converted to Christianity in order to obtain a Government position. The society set its aims high: to establish schools and colleges for the Jews, to promote among them arts and crafts, agriculture, and scientific pursuits, even to instil in them the laws of good breeding. It had but scant idea, however, how to achieve its aims, and accomplished very little in the few years of its existence.

The collapse of the Kulturverein was a severe blow to those Jews who were hoping to obtain full emancipation through a change of public opinion in favour of the Jews. Some of the members of the society—notably Gans and Heine—gave up the struggle in despair and went over to Christianity. Most of the rest fell back on the Reform movement, but rather as a *pis aller* than with any confidence. Salvation, however, came from an unexpected quarter. A young advocate named Gabriel Riesser(1806-1863), who hitherto had shown no interest in Judaism or its affairs, suddenly in 1831 took up with ardour the cause of Jewish emancipation, because he had himself been refused a post on the ground that he was a Jew. With great power and eloquence he demanded that equality of rights should be granted to the Jews as human beings, without any sacrifice of their religion being required of them. Largely through his efforts the tide of public opinion began to set in favour of Jewish emancipation, though the struggle had to last for several years yet. Riesser soon after began to take an active part in the affairs of the Hamburg Temple, becoming one of its presidents. He thus showed that he regarded Reform as the proper form of Judaism for the Jew to whom equality of civic rights was a matter of prime interest.

The Reform movement in Germany served as a model for a similar movement in England. Up to about the end of the Napoleonic wars the Jews of this country had been little touched by the "enlightenment" movement, and their Judaism remained completely of the old type. About this time some of the younger members began to agitate for a more decorous and attractive synagogue service, but for a long time those in authority would make no concessions or only very inadequate ones. Meanwhile a desire began to spread for more far-reaching changes, and in 1836 a number of members of the senior synagogue in London, the Spanish and Portuguese Congregation (so-called because it had been founded by the descendants of Jewish refugees from Spain and Portugal) petitioned the authorities for the introduction into the service "of such alterations and modifications as were in the line of the changes introduced into the Reform Synagogue in Hamburg and other places."

For some years after there was great friction between the two parties. The authorities still showed themselves averse to

THE EARLY REFORM MOVEMENT 121

making concessions, and in 1840 twenty-four prominent members of the London community resolved to organize themselves into a separate community. In 1842 they opened a new place of worship under the title of "The West London Synagogue of British Jews."[1] with a service modelled on that of the Hamburg Temple, though it retained rather more Hebrew, and also the prayers for the return to Zion and the coming of the Messiah, though not those for the restoration of the sacrificial cult.

In England, however, as in Germany, the essence of reform was the repudiation of Rabbinical authority; in his inaugural sermon in the West London Synagogue the Rev. D. W. Marks stated categorically that they did not place the traditions written in the Mishnah and Talmud on the same level with the Written Law contained in the Pentateuch, though they could use them as a guide.

In proclaiming the superiority of the Written over the Oral Law the Reformers were in appearance treading in the footsteps of the Karaites in the ninth century (vide Chapter iii). But there was a great difference between the spirit of their reform and that of Karaism. The Karaites had attached as much importance to ceremonial as the Rabbanites, only they sought for its detailed regulations not in the Talmud but in the Scriptures. But the modern Reformers, while still keeping much of the ceremonial, held it in far lower esteem than the orthodox Jews, and the chief reason why they refused to consider the Oral Law as binding was precisely because it attached so much importance to ceremonial.

It might be said that the essence of the new reform was to alter the long-standing relationship in the Jewish scheme of values between holiness and righteousness. In the Old Testament these two concepts vie with one another as ideals of conduct, "holiness" (Heb. *kedushah*) being concerned primarily with man's behaviour towards God, and "righteousness" (Heb. *tzedakah*) with his behaviour towards his fellow-men. Holiness, which comprised the whole of the ceremonial law,

---

[1] One reason for choosing the title "British" was that they included both "Spanish" and "German" Jews who differed somewhat in their liturgy (vide supra, p. 84).

including that of the sexual relationship, was the special concern of the priests, righteousness of the prophets. As we might expect, therefore, in the prophetical books and in the Psalms greater emphasis is laid upon righteousness.

In the Pentateuch there is an oscillation from one to the other, and in fact the distinction between them is somewhat blurred, as is shown by the fact that the regulations in the nineteenth chapter of Leviticus which are in the main a code of righteousness are introduced by the formula "Ye shall be holy."

Rabbinic Judaism in this respect followed the Pentateuch. It emphasizes the claims now of righteousness, now of holiness, and holds both in equal reverence. But the Reformers followed the line of the prophets, and came down decisively on the side of righteousness. "Returning to the Bible" for them meant deposing the Oral Law not so much in favour of the Written Law as of the prophets and Psalms. Holiness as an ideal ceased to have any attraction for them, and its law was obeyed, in so far as it was obeyed, chiefly for sentimental or hygienic reasons. This was especially noticeable in the matter of forbidden foods. The section on unclean foods in the Pentateuch closes with the words "Ye shall strive after holiness and be holy" (Lev. xi, 44). This was enough for the orthodox Jew. But the Reformer, even if he observed these precepts, would justify his conduct as beneficial to health. The idea of holiness, like the hope of a return to Zion, ceased to influence his conduct.

Along with the authority of the Oral Law the Reform Movement discarded entirely the study of the Talmud and with it to a large extent that of the Hebrew language. It retained a good deal of Hebrew in the service "for old times' sake." But it read its Bible in German or English, and looked for the elucidation of the text not to the Hebrew commentators but to the sermon in the vernacular.

Not all Jews who sought to modernize themselves concurred in the Reform conception of Judaism. Certainly they could no longer attach the same sanctity to the Talmud and the Zohar as the old-fashioned Jew. But there were those to whom the Hebrew language was still dear and the Jewish past a source of pride and inspiration. They saw no reason why an Hebraic

THE EARLY REFORM MOVEMENT 123

culture at any rate should be incompatible with either enlightenment or emancipation. This cultural element in Judaism, which had been overlooked by Furtado and his associates, was made by these men the basis of a new form of the Jewish religion which combined acceptance of the duties of citizenship with strong attachment to Jewish tradition.

This new kind of Judaism took up a position intermediate between the old-fashioned orthodoxy of the ghetto and the new-fangled reform. It differed essentially from the former in the fact that, like the *haskalah* in East Europe, it gave precedence to the study of the Bible over that of the Talmud. But it studied the Bible in Hebrew, basing its interpretation on the *biur* of the Mendelssohnian school (*vide supra*, p. 101). While not making Hebrew its cultural language, like the *haskalah*, it retained a strong affection for that language, which led it to devote much attention to post-biblical Hebrew literature, including, of course, the Talmud and Midrash; and this study in turn kept them on the whole faithful to the traditional observance of Judaism and the orthodox form of service.

To these intermediate Jews the use of the sermon in the vernacular was no less indispensable than it was to the Reform Jews as an instrument for combining Jewish and civic loyalty. But they could not be so insensible as were the reformers to the strong objection of the old-fashioned ghetto Jews to the introduction of such sermons into the synagogue service. Of particular value to them therefore was the publication in 1832 of Leopold Zunz's *Gottesdienstliche Vorträge der Juden* ("The Sermon in the Jewish Synagogue Service"), though it was not written specially for their benefit.

In this work Zunz showed that addresses in the vernacular had from a very early period been an essential feature of Jewish religious life, contributing greatly to the moral and intellectual welfare of the people, and that there could be no religious objection against them. Largely in consequence of Zunz's work the sermon did not remain a monopoly of the reformers, but became an integral part of the orthodox service also.

The Hebraic reaction may be said to have commenced with the appearance in 1821 of the first number of a magazine entitled *Der Bibelsche Orient*. This publication adopted the standpoint that, while it was right that the Jews should strive for enlightenment and political emancipation, they had no reason to be ashamed of their past, and it was wrong of them to neglect their own literary treasures and the religious and ethical teaching which they embodied. Like Lessing in his *Erziehung des Menschengeschlechts*, it laid stress on the historical role played by the Jewish people in the spiritual and intellectual development of humanity, thus breaking away from Mendelssohn, who had found himself unable to accept Lessing's views on this point.

Carrying this idea further, it maintained that the Jewish people still had the task of bringing mankind back to God. The first requisite for their fulfilling this task was that they should bring themselves back to God; and for this purpose it was necessary that they should study the Bible in the original Hebrew. The Talmud and Cabbalah might also be useful, but of these the writer was more critical.

The *Bibelscher Orient* appeared anonymously, but its authorship was commonly ascribed to Isaac Bernays (1792–1849), a gifted preacher who had recently been appointed Rabbi—or, as he preferred to call himself, Chakham—of the orthodox community in Hamburg. Bernays himself disclaimed the authorship of the *Orient*, but both in word and in deed he showed obvious marks of its inspiration. As head of an important section of the Hamburg community, he made it his object to Germanize its members while at the same time keeping alive their Jewish self-consciousness and their attachment to their people and religion.

To achieve this purpose Bernays made changes both within and without the synagogue. In the synagogue he introduced greater order and decorum into the service and made the German sermon an integral part of it. Outside the synagogue he devoted particular attention to the education of the young. Hitherto in the *talmud torah*, or elementary Jewish school attached to the synagogue, the only subjects taught had been Hebrew and arithmetic. Bernays transformed it into a thoroughly modern school in which Hebrew and Jewish subjects had an important place in the curriculum.

Another pioneer of this form of Judaism was Isaac Noah

Mannheimer (1793–1865), from Copenhagen, who became Rabbi of the Vienna community in 1824. Though imbued with the same ideas as Bernays, Mannheimer made greater concessions to the progressive element in order to avoid a split in the community. He rendered the service more aesthetic, and allowed the synagogue to be called a "Temple." While Bernays condemned unreservedly a new prayer book issued by the Hamburg Temple community in 1841, Mannheimer found much to say in its favour, though like Bernays he objected to the omission of the references to the Messiah and the national restoration of Israel.

The services instituted by Bernays and Mannheimer were taken as a model by numerous communities in Western Europe and America. Prominent among those who continued their work was the Bohemian-born Michael Sachs (1808–1864), a gifted preacher and accomplished Hebrew scholar, who was Rabbi of the chief Berlin congregation from 1844 until he resigned sooner than allow an organ to be introduced into the synagogue. Thanks to the efforts of Bernays, Mannheimer and Sachs, and others of like mind—conspicuous among whom was the great Italian Hebraist, Samuel David Luzzatto (head of the Rabbinical Seminary at Padua)—orthodoxy remained a living force among the Jews outside the Ghetto in Western Europe, and the services which they instituted were largely taken as a model, and attracted more worshippers than the Reform services.

Compared with the old-fashioned orthodox services they were themselves reformed. But they retained what might be called the orthodox atmosphere. In the Reform service the basic language, so to speak, was the vernacular, even if it occupied only a small part of the service, while Hebrew was in the position of a "tolerated" language. In the orthodox service the relation was reversed; Hebrew was the native and the vernacular the intruder.

Among the Germanized Jews the reaction against reform was carried to its furthest point by Samson Rafael Hirsch (1808–1888) of Hamburg. In his childhood Hirsch was a pupil of Bernays, and from him and from his home training he imbibed a strong affection for orthodox Judaism, which was only confirmed by his experiences as a student at Bonn University. Without being a great scholar or thinker, Hirsch had a strong appreciation of moral values, and he found the ideal moral discipline in the Mosaic law, particularly the ceremonial part of it. The *mitzvah* became precious in his eyes as a means of curbing the passions without suppressing the *joie de vivre*. He therefore made his rule of life the strictest adherence to the Shulchan Aruch—the orthodox code—in all its minutiae, while cultivating a modern outlook on all worldly subjects.

Hirsch became Rabbi of one of the Frankfort congregations in 1851, and he succeeded in impressing on it his own character. His type of Judaism came to be known as neo-orthodoxy, from its close resemblance to the old orthodoxy of the Ghetto, from which, however, it differed somewhat in spirit. It laid the same emphasis on the *mitzvah*, but rather for its moral value in this world than as a passport to the next.

The "Frankfort Chassidim" (Pietists), as they came to be called, and those who copied them in other countries, were distinguished among Western Jews for their punctilious performance of the precepts of Jewish law. But in their opinions they were sometimes very free. It was action which counted with them, and so long as this was on the right lines their conscience was satisfied.

Hirsch paid particular attention to the subject of education. He founded in Frankfort a school in which a high standard was set both in Jewish and non-Jewish subjects, and which won commendation from many who did not agree with his views. His following, which had been considerable in his lifetime, fell off somewhat after his death, but remained predominant in his own city of Frankfort.

CHAPTER XII

THE ADVANCED REFORM MOVEMENT

THE controversy between the "Reform" Jews and the orthodox or even semi-orthodox in the early decades of the nineteenth century had concerned itself only with the authority of the Talmud. This was discarded wholly by the Reformers and partially by the conservatives, while it was maintained in its integrity by the old-fashioned orthodox. All three sections, however, concurred in recognizing the inspiration of the Bible and the binding character of the Mosaic legislation contained in it; even the Reformers found such an attitude compatible both with "enlightenment" and with "emancipation."

In the middle decades of the nineteenth century new forms of Judaism came into being in which the Bible no longer enjoyed this position of pre-eminence. The spirit of the age was against acknowledging religious authority of any sort; and naturally the Jews of Western Europe did not remain unaffected by it. There were now many Jews, especially in Germany, the great home of Jewish intellectualism, who followed with keen interest the development of modern thought, and who considered it incumbent on them, as members of a civilized society, to be thoroughly modern in their outlook and ideas. This process involved in most cases a certain revision of their ideas with regard to the Bible; and the question arose for them whether such revision entailed any change in their relation to Judaism also.

The way to this new development was paved by the growth in the early part of the nineteenth century of a new method of Jewish study which came to be known as Jüdische Wissenschaft, or Jewish Science. The essence of this method was the application to the Jewish past, especially since the beginning of the Christian era, of modern methods of historical inquiry and research. Up to the beginning of the nineteenth century such methods had been totally unknown to the students of the Talmud who, in the seclusion of the *beth hamidrash*, remained almost completely unaware of the distinction between past and present in Jewish life and of the changes which had taken place in the world around them.

The first talmudical students to emerge from this kind of dreamland and to view the Jewish past objectively were Nachman Krochmal (*vide supra*, Chapter viii) and his disciple, Solomon Rapaport of Lemberg (1790–1867), who became the pioneers of research on modern lines into Jewish history.

It was, however, a German scholar who transformed this research into a definite branch of study. This was Leopold Zunz (1794–1886), one of the original founders of the ill-starred Berlin Culturverein (*vide*, p. 119). Unlike Gans and Heine, Zunz was led by the failure of the Culturverein not to despair of Judaism but to seek for some new way of saving it; and for this purpose he took up and developed the research work of Krochmal and Rapaport with which he was already acquainted. He showed how such research could bring to light what may be called Jewish values—moral, intellectual and aesthetic—and so made Jüdische Wissenschaft an instrument for combating both anti-Jewish prejudice outside the community and obscurantism within.

A new significance was given to research into the Jewish past by Abraham Geiger of Frankfort (1810–1875), one of the central figures of German Jewry in the nineteenth century. After receiving a good Hebrew education at home, Geiger became a distinguished Orientalist, and he early conceived a great admiration for Zunz, whose work in the field of Jüdische Wissenschaft he aspired to continue. He was, however, young enough to fall under the spell of new ideas just coming into vogue to which Zunz was on the whole impervious.

One of these was the notion—unknown to the rationalistic age of Mendelssohn—of progress and development in the history of man. The achievements of modern civilization were now coming to be regarded as the culmination of a long and continuous process, which was destined to lead mankind to still higher levels. It was becoming almost a commonplace of

THE ADVANCED REFORM MOVEMENT 129

thought that man was not only a rational but also a progressive animal, and that his present condition and future prospects should be considered from that point of view. This notion was profoundly influencing research in all branches of inquiry, and at an early period determined Geiger's approach to the study of Jüdische Wissenschaft.

Geiger's new departure was to regard Jewish history itself in its totality as an example of development and evolution. Judaism had hitherto been a religion of law; it was now time that it evolved into one of monotheistic belief. He was sure that in so doing Judaism would be following the line of its own development; but his endeavours to prove this point are not without embarrassment.

He divides Jewish history up to the time of Mendelssohn into three periods. The first he calls the period of revelation; this was the creative period during which the law took shape in its main outlines. The second period was that of tradition, when a great deal of floating matter left from the previous period was given definite form and added to the previous body of law. The third period was that of rigid legality, when the whole body of law handed down from the two previous periods was sedulously preserved and practised.

With Mendelssohn, according to Geiger, commenced the fourth epoch, that of criticism. How the transition was made to this epoch from its predecessor, suddenly as it were and without preparation, Geiger confesses is a mystery to him. "So it is, in fact," he says; "one cannot see the paths pursued by history, yet the change suddenly becomes visible." Like Mendelssohn, Geiger holds that the monotheistic idea can and ought to be discovered by the unassisted human reason through the study of philosophy, albeit a somewhat different philosophy from that of Mendelssohn, and one which led to a theistic rather than deistic conception of God. But unlike Mendelssohn, he holds that the only element in traditional Judaism worth preserving is its theology, by which he meant its universalistic monotheism, with its corresponding ethical system. The rest may have been good in its time, but was no longer needed by the modern Jew, in fact, it was a positive hindrance to his spiritual development. Jewish history, he held, should be

I

studied with a view to finding out the place occupied by the monotheistic idea in the life of the Jewish people at any given period and separating it from the adventitious elements by which it was encompassed.

He himself provided an example of this method in his best-known work, *Urschrift und Uebersetzungen der Bibel*, in which among other things he showed that the talmudical authorities themselves had made changes in the original text of the Hebrew Scriptures in order to bring it abreast of the theological ideas of their own age.

Geiger's notion that in discarding Jewish religious practices he was following the line of Jewish evolution is obviously based on a very arbitrary interpretation of Jewish history. One may surmise that in adopting such an interpretation he was influenced subconsciously by other than purely intellectual considerations. Besides being a student and a scholar, Geiger was also an orator with a fine sense of style and an excellent command of the German language. He was equally at home with the pen, on the lecture platform, and in the pulpit. He was also qualified to shine in society and not devoid of social ambitions. Such a man would naturally be biased in favour of a conception of Judaism which allowed him the greatest freedom to assimilate to his non-Jewish surroundings and to mix freely with them.

While Geiger was perhaps the first preacher of assimilation to the Jews of Germany, the chief apostle of this movement was a man of somewhat different attainments and character, though of no less ability. Samuel Holdheim (1806–1862) was born at Kempen in Polish Prussia, where in his early years he had received an exclusively talmudic education and had become highly proficient in talmudic casuistry. Like many other Polish Jews from the time of Moses Mendelssohn and even earlier, he had been impelled by his thirst for more general knowledge to wander into Germany, though a desire to improve his material position had also no doubt weighed equally with him.

In Germany he cultivated the art of pulpit oratory with great success, and became a "Reform" Minister or Rabbi. When, however, Geiger began to publish his ideas on Jewish religious development in the *Zeitschrift für jüdische Theologie* which he founded in 1836, Holdheim took them up with enthusiasm and himself wrote articles embodying the same conception of Judaism.

It was not long before the fruits of such teaching began to show themselves. By this time the battle of political emancipation for the Jews had practically been won, even in Germany, and they could look beyond equality of rights to attaining social equality as well. Naturally they found the obligations of the Jewish law a great hindrance to them in this endeavour.

In 1842 a number of educated Jewish laymen in Germany formed themselves into a "Union of the Friends of Reform" (*Verein der Reformfreunde*), which in a declaration issued in the October of that year repudiated the authority of the Talmud and expressed the opinion that "the Mosaic religion was capable of continuous development." On the strength of this view they declared themselves free from the dietary laws, which "as a religious act or symbol had lost their significance," and they rejected the messianic hope on the ground that "they looked upon the land of their birth as their only fatherland."

The Verein went on to declare the rite of circumcision to be optional. This was more than even the most advanced of the Reform section were as yet prepared for, and led to the break-up of the Verein. But the spiritual unrest of which the manifesto was a sign persisted and produced further developments. In June 1844 twenty-three of the younger Rabbis, mostly from south and west Germany, met in Brunswick to deliberate on the best method of bringing Jewish theory and practice into accord with the requirements of German citizenship. The conference was dominated by Holdheim, who seized the opportunity to win acceptance for his own ideas of Judaism.

He made his starting-point the distinction drawn in the declaration of the Paris Sanhedrin between the religious-ethical and the national-political aspects of Judaism, and like the Sanhedrin declared the latter to be abrogated. But, in accordance with the new theory that the Jewish religion was capable of development and evolution, he gave to this element a much wider scope than the Sanhedrin had done. He made it include everything in Judaism which was inconvenient to "German citizens of the Jewish persuasion" who desired to mix freely with their fellow-Germans—Sabbath, marriage and dietary laws, and even the Hebrew language. He aimed at procuring for the Rabbi exactly the same civil status as that of the Christian minister, and on that ground protested vigorously against a decision of the Prussian Government to give the Rabbis a certain measure of autonomy in dealing with Jewish family matters.

The decisions of the Brunswick conference were confirmed by a much more imposing Rabbinical conference held at Frankfort in July 1845, where again Holdheim was the dominant figure. Soon after a new Temple was built in Berlin where he was installed as Rabbi and where his ideas were put into practice. A form of service was introduced which had little in common with that of the old-fashioned synagogue or *schule* of the Ghetto. Most of the prayers were in German and were not markedly Jewish in character; the one distinctively Jewish feature was the reading of a section of the Pentateuch in Hebrew. From the pulpit Holdheim proclaimed the abrogation of the whole ceremonial law, including also circumcision, which he declared to be optional; he even celebrated mixed marriages between Jews and non-Jews.

Not all the Rabbis who had taken part in the Frankfort conference went as far as Holdheim. Even Geiger, who at this time occupied a Rabbinic post at Breslau, considered his reforms as too radical, though he could hardly have denied that they were the logical application of his own theories. Even in its mildest shape, however, ultra-Reform was separated by a deep gulf from the old-fashioned Judaism. It appealed especially to the Jews who desired to assimilate themselves to their surroundings to the utmost degree without entirely severing their connection with Judaism.

The orthodox stigmatized it as a stepping-stone to Christianity, but it would be more correct to say that it provided a halting-place for many who without it would have joined the Church. That Holdheim succeeded in inspiring his congregation with an attachment to Judaism was proved by the fact that not one member of his congregation converted either himself or his children to Christianity.

Had the Jews of Germany been free to follow their own

THE ADVANCED REFORM MOVEMENT 133

bent, they would probably have established many synagogues after the model of Holdheim's. In many communities there were important sections which were anxious to adopt his reforms to a greater or less degree. They were, however, prevented from carrying out their desires by the refusal of the Prussian Government to recognize them if they broke away from the established form. After a brief period of liberalism, this Government had set its face against any change in the Jewish form of service, and for more than twenty years after in all the quarrels between the orthodox and reform parties it almost invariably took the side of the former.

In pursuance of this policy it had for a long time in 1839 refused the necessary naturalization to Geiger himself when he was appointed one of the Rabbis of the Breslau community, and in the end granted it only on condition that he should be subordinate to the orthodox Rabbi, to the great chagrin of the majority. But for this hostility the Jews of Berlin would not have had to wait till 1848 for their first reform synagogue.

One result of this attitude on the part of the Prussian Government was that a number of able men who either were or might have become Reform Rabbis in Germany emigrated to America. The New World at that time was attracting large numbers of liberal-minded Germans who sought to escape from the oppressive régime of their own country. Among them were many Jews whose religious views were as liberal as their political. In the communities founded by such men the Reform Rabbis had no difficulty in obtaining positions commensurate with their abilities; and they not only transplanted Reform Judaism to America but before long gave it a distinctly American character.

CHAPTER XIII

REFORM IN AMERICA—THE MISSION OF ISRAEL

THE German Reform Rabbis who migrated to America in the middle decades of the nineteenth century did not take with them a well-defined form of Judaism such as the orthodox possessed. The third, and last, of the great Rabbinic conferences, held at Breslau in 1846, had left many important questions undecided and on others had adopted a weak compromise so as not unduly to offend the orthodox. Hence much was still left to the discretion of the individual Rabbi. But broadly speaking they all adopted the evolutionary view of Judaism propounded by Geiger and Holdheim, and they were all strongly assimilationist in tendency—that is, they sought in every way to remove the barriers to social intercourse between Jew and non-Jew, and courted above all things the good opinion of the non-Jewish world.

Each, however, had his own way of putting these principles into practice; and, as America was the land of experiment, they were on the whole allowed a free hand by their congregations to fashion Judaism according to their own ideas. The result was that for a time there was great diversity in Reform practice in America. Each Rabbi had his own form of prayer and his own *minhag* (ceremonial), and each defined Jewish doctrine in his own way. They were all, however, in agreement on one fundamental point—that nothing was to stand in the way of their becoming thoroughly American, and that no sacrifice of Jewish tradition could be too great for this end.

In the second half of the century a considerable measure of uniformity was introduced into American Reform Judaism, chiefly through the efforts of one man. Isaac Mayer Wise

(1819–1900) was born in Bohemia and became in his early years a qualified orthodox Rabbi. After acting for a few years in that capacity in Radunitz in Bohemia, he emigrated in 1846 to the United States, where he was able to give free rein to his leanings towards reform. He eventually became Rabbi in Cincinnati, a city which contained perhaps the most cultured and important settlement of Germans, both non-Jewish and Jewish, in the States.

Wise's chief talent lay in the field of organization, and he worked with a great deal of success to bring order and shape into the Reform movement of America. Chiefly through his efforts a conference of Reform Rabbis and lay leaders was held at Cleveland in 1855. This paved the way for a purely Rabbinic conference at Philadelphia in 1869, presided over by Wise himself, where a definite programme of Reform was laid down and adopted by the leading Reform Rabbis of America.

This programme can best be described by quoting the resolutions of the Conference almost *in extenso*. They were as follows:

1. "The Messianic aim of Judaism is not the restoration of the old Jewish state under a descendant of David, involving a second separation from the nations of the earth, but the union of all children of God in confession of the unity of God, so as to realize the unity of all rational creatures and call to moral sanctification.

2. "We look on the destruction of the second Jewish commonwealth not as a punishment for the sinfulness of Israel, but as a result of the divine purpose revealed to Abraham, which, as has become more clear in the course of world history, consists in the dispersion of the Jews to all parts of the earth, for the realization of their high-priestly mission, to lead nations to a true knowledge and worship of God.

3. "The Aaronic priesthood and Mosaic sacrificial cult were preparatory steps to a real priesthood of the whole people, which began with the dispersal of Jews, and to the sacrifices of sincere devotion and moral sanctification which alone are pleasing and acceptable to the Most Holy. These institutions, preparatory to higher religiosity, were consigned to the past once and for all with the destruction of the second Temple, and only in this

sense—as educational influences in the past—are they to be mentioned in prayer.

4. "Every distinction between Aaronides and non-Aaronides, as far as religious rites and duties are concerned, is consequently inadmissible, both in religious and social life.

5. "The selection of Israel as the people of religion, as the bearer of the highest idea of humanity, is still as ever to be strongly emphasized, and for this very reason, whenever this is mentioned, it shall be done with full emphasis laid on the world-embracing mission of Israel and the love of God for all his children.

6. "The belief in a bodily resurrection has no religious foundation, and the doctrine of immortality refers to the after existence of the soul only.

7. "Urgently as the cultivation of the Hebrew language must be desired as the fulfilment of a sacred duty, it has become unintelligible to most of our co-religionists and must give way in prayer to an intelligible language."

A second Rabbinic conference held at Pittsburgh in 1885 repeated these points in a more concise form, and added the following further points of importance:

1. "The Bible reflects primitive ideas of its own age, clothing conceptions of divine Providence and Justice in miraculous narratives.

2. "We accept as binding only the moral laws of the Mosaic code and maintain ceremonies which elevate and sanctify life, but reject all such as are not adapted to the views and habits of modern civilization.

3. "The laws regulating diet, priestly purity and dress do not conduce to holiness and obstruct modern spiritual elevation.

4. "We are no longer a nation but a spiritual community and therefore expect no return to Palestine.

5. "In accordance with the spirit of the Mosaic legislation we deem it our duty to solve on the basis of justice and righteousness the problems presented by the contrasts and evils of the present organization of society."

The resolutions of the Pittsburgh Conference became the recognized basis of the Reform movement in America. The uniformity thus established was confirmed by further steps due directly or indirectly to the influence of Wise. In 1873 he organized the Union of American Congregations—the original number was thirty-four, which in half a century had grown to nearly three hundred—and this body in 1875 founded the Hebrew Union College for the training of Reform Rabbis, an institution which gradually produced a class of American Reform Rabbis with a common training and outlook. Wise also organized in 1889 the Central Conference of American Rabbis as a permanent body meeting annually; one of the first fruits of its labours was a Union Prayer Book which already in 1904 was in use in 158 congregations.

The resolutions of the Philadelphia and Pittsburgh Conferences, like those of the Frankfort Conference of 1845, show clearly the inspiration of Geiger. They are based on Geiger's postulate that the Jews are a religious community, that the essence of Judaism is its theology, and that the law is merely a stage in the evolution of Judaism.

This theology found its most complete exposition in a book called *Outlines of a Systematic Theology of Judaism*, written by Rabbi Kaufman Kohler, head of the Hebrew Union College, and first published (in German) in 1910. It consists of a number of propositions regarding God and man and the relations between them belonging to the system of thought which we might call theistic unitarianism or unitarian theism. Kohler, however, is at pains to prove—and with some success—that all of them can be found in recognized Jewish sources; and for this reason his theology may with some justification call itself Jewish.

But granting that its theology is Jewish, this religion is in no sense a religion of *torah*. If it at all finds divine guidance in the Bible, it is not in the Pentateuch, but in certain passages of the Prophets and Psalms. It might even be regarded as a rival to the religion of *torah*. From their insistence on the ideas of "holiness" and "sanctification," it is obvious that the Rabbis of the Philadelphia Conference had in their minds the statement which in the Pentateuch heralds the revelation on Mount Sinai: "Ye shall be to Me a kingdom of priests and a holy nation." Obviously they believed that this, or something very much like it, was still the goal of the Jewish people.

But they held that the goal should be attained in quite a different way. The Pentateuch had prescribed for this purpose the "law of holiness." The Reform Rabbis swept this away and put in its place what they called "the mission of Israel," that is, a kind of missionary zeal on the part of the Jews to disseminate the Reform theology.

A good idea of this missionary spirit may be derived from the following prayer included in the prayer book composed by Rabbi David Einhorn, Kohler's father-in-law, which was made the basis of the prayer book of the United American Reform Congregations: "Arm us, our Guardian and Protector, with strength and love for our exalted mission, so that Thy light may rise for all the sons of man and Israel's progeny become numerous like the stars of heaven. Make all sections of our race recognize the exalted goal of its vicissitudes and struggles in exile. A tragic cleft traverses the House of Jacob. His children are divided between a dying world which assigns to him the destiny of dwelling perpetually alone and isolated among the nations, and a newly arising world, which, urged by the spirit of Thy prophets, sees its highest glory and achievement in the union of all Thy children with the people of Thy covenant . . . Enlighten all who are called by Thy name with the knowledge that . . . in the same moment when the gates of his ancient temple were closed, Thou didst open to him the gates of the world, in order that Thy kingdom may embrace the whole world and Thy people encompass all peoples."[1]

This notion of the "mission of Israel" is what chiefly distinguished the "Reform" of America and its Rabbis from that of Geiger and Germany. In content their religion was the same, and both believed that it had a value for the world at large. But while the Germans were content to affirm this among themselves, the Americans proclaimed it from the housetops. This missionary zeal seems to have been inspired by a somewhat mystical reading of the prophetical books of the Old Testament, and its seeds had already been sown in Germany. In that country, however, conditions were adverse to its development, and it was only in the free atmosphere of America that it could come to full fruition.

[1] Quoted by Kohler, op. cit.

It was in England that Liberal Judaism found its most earnest apostle, in the person of Claude Montefiore (1858-1935), one of the leaders of Anglo-Jewry. Montefiore's parents belonged to the West London Congregation of British Jews (*vide supra*, p. 121), and he himself, being of a deeply religious temperament, originally intended to become a Minister there, though possessed of independent means.

With this end in view, after studying at Oxford, where he came under the influence of Jowett, he read theology for a time in Germany. Here he imbibed the theological doctrines of the Geiger school, and completely outgrew the moderate and old-fashioned reform of the West London Synagogue. In 1892 he delivered the Hibbert Lectures on the religious development of Israel as portrayed in the Old Testament, which he conceived of as a basis for still further development. By this time he had become deeply imbued with the idea of the "mission of Israel," which, like the American Rabbis, he derived from his interpretation of the history of the Jewish people.

Early in the present century he became president of a new movement called "The Jewish Religious Union," which in due course developed into the first organized Liberal Jewish group in England. In 1911 he published a kind of manual of Liberal Judaism for the use of parents and teachers, and soon afterwards under his auspices a Liberal Synagogue was opened in London, the weekly services at which were held on Sunday and were of the same type as those of Holdheim's Temple in Berlin.

Montefiore's Liberal Judaism as revealed in his book on the subject was essentially the same as that of the American Reform Rabbis, but it was set forth by him much more clearly and incisively—without, one might say, either the German pomposity or the American effusiveness. He had the courage of his convictions and was not afraid to commit himself to statements which might startle even Liberal Jews who had not fully thought out their position. "The Jews," he maintains, as a cardinal doctrine of his religion, "have been chosen by God to exercise in divers ways, directly or indirectly, an important influence upon a great section of humanity . . . in the direction of a gradual diffusion of certain doctrines about God and righteousness, and about the relation of man to God and of God to man," some of which he attempts to set forth. To this true doctrine, however, must be added true *experience* about the same subjects. Experience he defines as "making religion something which is felt and lived"; and this is the very essence of the Jewish mission, that the Jews should both cultivate this experience themselves and diffuse it among others.

About the missionary character of his Judaism Montefiore has no qualms: "Christianity itself," he says, "seems to Jews only a stage in the preparation of the world for a purified, developed, and universalized Judaism."

But is it Judaism? In being "purified, developed and universalized," does not the religion of *torah* lose everything which makes it distinctively Jewish? Montefiore is not unaware of this objection and states it quite fairly. "There are Jews," he says, "who declare that 'Liberal' Judaism has no connection with history, that it is un-Jewish, that it has cut itself off from the past, and that it is a mere vague Theism which will soon entirely lose its slight Jewish veneer" (Chapter xviii). Instead, however, of even attempting to answer this criticism, he goes off into other matters. None the less, he seems to have felt the force of it; in his later years he took certain steps to make the "Jewish veneer" a little thicker, and since his death this process has been carried further; thus the main weekly service at the Liberal Synagogue is now no longer on Sunday but on Saturday, the Jewish Sabbath.

Apart from this, Liberal Judaism on its ethical side has remained strictly Jewish. While free from prejudice against the New Testament, it has continued to derive its ethical ideals from the Old Testament, with frequent resort to the teaching of the Rabbis. In this way it has maintained the tradition of the original reform movement in England (*vide*, p. 121) about the Jewishness of which there could be no question.

CHAPTER XIV

THE HISTORICAL SCHOOL

LIBERAL Judaism aimed among other things at breaking down the barriers created by religion between Jews and non-Jews. It is true that Liberal Jews continued to speak of the old-fashioned Rabbinically-orthodox Jews as their "co-religionists," but they could with more justice have applied this term to Unitarians of the school of James Martineau. Certainly they had quite as strong a feeling of solidarity with their fellow-nationals of England or America as with their so-called co-religionists of the Russian Pale. In proportion as they became Americanized or Anglicized they also became de-Judaized.

No doubt they could justify this change in their own mind on the ground that it was an essential part of the "mission of Israel," without which they could not hope to carry out their task of bringing the rest of the world over to a kind of Judaism. But it was obvious that the attempt to do so under such conditions involved them in the danger of themselves being absorbed by their surroundings and cut off from the Jewish people.

Liberal Judaism was a logical outcome of two impulses derived by the modern Jew from his environment—to reject authority in religious matters and to apply to the Jewish religion the principle of development and progress. No doubt it was some presentiment of what these impulses might lead to that caused S. R. Hirsch to suppress them forcibly by means of a rigid formalism. But there were others who found means of giving them free play without endangering their own organic connection with the Jewish people.

They maintained that connection by loyalty to the Jewish *tradition*, which was completely disregarded by the Liberal Jews. Not that they followed this tradition blindly and unquestioningly, like the orthodox Jews. They recognized in it a principle, not indeed of evolution but of adaptation to changing circumstances, and distinguished its various elements according to the times when they were introduced and for which they were originally intended. But they found in it much that was of value at the present day, if for no other reason than because it inspired those who followed it with a certain Jewish self-consciousness and formed a link for them between the present and the past. It was this which distinguished them sharply from the Liberal Jews. They took an interest in the Jewish past for its own sake, and not merely as the seed-ground for the monotheistic idea. On this account they were known as the historical school.

The historical approach to Judaism grew naturally out of Zunz's Jüdische Wissenschaft, and Zunz himself was one of its prominent representatives in his later years. The first, however, to take it up systematically was Zacharias Frankel (1801–1875), of Prague, who is usually regarded as the founder of the historical school.

Like Geiger, Frankel was both a student of Jüdische Wissenschaft and a Rabbi, though he was better versed in the Talmud than Geiger. As Rabbi of Dresden, Frankel had adopted a policy of moderate reform similar to that of Mannheimer (*vide*, p. 125). He had in consequence been invited to attend the Frankfort Rabbinical Conference in 1845 (*vide*, p. 132). There he had been shocked by the proposal that the use of Hebrew should practically be discarded both in the synagogue and the home, and after raising his voice in energetic protest had left the conference. This incident led him to prosecute his historical studies with renewed energy, with a view to justifying the position he had taken up.

The fruit of his labours was seen in a Hebrew book called *Ways of the Mishnah*, published in 1857, in which he traced historically the growth and compilation of that work. His chief object was to correlate the Mishnah not with the development of Jewish theology, as Geiger had done, but with the history of the Jewish people. This approach to Hebrew literature, which soon found many followers, led him to adopt a form of Judaism similar to that of Bernays and Mannheimer,

THE HISTORICAL SCHOOL 143

but rather more flexible and allowing more scope for individual judgment.

In 1854 Frankel was appointed head of the newly established Breslau Rabbinical Seminary, in preference to Geiger, to whose initiative the foundation of the Seminary was largely due. In this position he inculcated what he called "positive historical Judaism," as a kind of counterblast to the theological Judaism of Geiger. Apparently he meant to indicate by this title that Geiger's historical researches were negative, and aimed at eliminating the influence of the Jewish past on its present, whereas his own were positive and aimed at maintaining that influence as far as possible.

He found an able supporter in the most brilliant of his colleagues at Breslau, Heinrich Graetz (1817-1888). Born in the province of Posen, where the Jews were still more of the Polish than of the German type, Graetz had been given a good grounding in Talmud and Hebrew, and he always retained a warm affection for these subjects. Later he devoted his chief attention to history in general and Jewish history in particular.

On the opening of the Breslau Seminary he was appointed Lecturer in Jewish History there, a position which he held till his death. Adopting Frankel's "positive historical" approach to Judaism, he was able, in virtue of his literary gifts, to give it a far wider popular appeal. He aimed particularly at strengthening the "Selbstgefühl," the Jewish consciousness, of the Jews of Germany, and it was chiefly with this object in view that he composed his monumental *Geschichte der Juden* (History of the Jews), commenced in 1855 and concluded in 1874, and covering the whole history of the Jewish people in eleven volumes, up to 1848. The first to appear in 1855 was Vol. III, on the period after the destruction of the Second Temple (i.e. the Talmudic period).

Graetz set out to write the history of the Jews as a people, that is, as a social group united by ties of blood, and by common traditions and customs, and therefore possessing a distinctive past, a distinctive religion, and a distinctive language. As such they could rank with the other peoples of the world, and their history was part of world history. Having thus what might be called a national history of their own—even if they were no longer a nation in the full sense—the Jews had no need to merge themselves in the peoples among whom they lived. They could co-operate with them in the political, economic, social and cultural fields, while yet retaining their own individuality.

As a people the Jews had a right to that individuality, like any other people, wherever they might be living. This is the lesson which stands out from Graetz's treatment of Jewish history as a whole and of each section and period of it in detail.

It is a natural inference from this view that the best form of the Jewish religion for the modern world is one that helps the Jew to preserve his individuality without hindering his activities as a citizen. It is not difficult to see where Graetz found such a form. He protests strongly against Geiger's reduction of Judaism to a mere religion and speaks with abhorrence of Holdheim's extreme reforms. On the other hand he has no sympathy with the formalism of S. R. Hirsch, which he dismisses as "mummy worship." But he speaks with almost lyrical enthusiasm of Mannheimer and Sachs, the men who retained the traditional spirit of Judaism under a modernized exterior. In view therefore of the great popularity which Graetz's History attained both in Germany and other countries, he may be considered one of the principal champions of conservative Judaism.

Frankel and Graetz might with justice claim that in pointing out the value of the traditional Jewish religion for strengthening Jewish self-consciousness they had made it compatible with a modern outlook. The vital principle in that religion, however, was the particularistic faith from which it had sprung—the faith in the God of Israel. When abandoning that faith Geiger and his followers were perfectly consistent in abandoning with it the traditional religion. Graetz might scoff at Geiger for reducing Judaism to a mere theology; but that theology, with its purely universalistic conception of God, was his theology also. This is shown partly by his rejection of the idea of a personal Messiah, but even more by his disbelief in the inspiration of the Bible, which he surveyed from the "higher critical" standpoint.

His observance in practice was thus combined with scepticism in theory. This inconsistency naturally did not escape the

Liberal Jews, and Montefiore was able to retort upon the "historicals" that "observances which run counter to faith, which violate a cherished belief, or which are not based upon belief, have no religious value any longer."[1]

The force of this criticism was strongly felt by one of the leading "historicals" of the generation after Graetz. Solomon Schechter (1847-1915) came from Rumania, where he had been brought up in a Chassidic milieu. After learning Talmud in his early years he had gone to Vienna and Berlin and there studied Jewish theology under Jewish scholars and philosophy at the University. In 1882 he came to England as tutor in Rabbinics to Claude Montefiore, through whose good offices he became Reader in Rabbinics at Cambridge in 1892. In 1901 he became head of the Jewish Theological Seminary in New York, which had been founded some years before by the conservative elements in American Jewry.

In the preface to his *Studies in Judaism*, published in 1896, Schechter somewhat humorously breaks a lance with his fellow-historicals over the rival claims of tradition and revelation. He calls the Synagogue of the Eastern Jews, in which he was himself brought up, the "Low Synagogue"—"a place of worship rather bare and bald, if not repulsive, frequented by a noisy and excitable people, who actually danced on the 'Season of Rejoicing' and cried bitterly on the 'Days of Mourning' "; while the more decorous synagogues of the modern orthodox with their "beauty of holiness" he designates "High Synagogue." While belonging now to the "High Synagogue" himself, he still feels a certain nostalgia for the old Low Synagogue, in which, "with all its attachment to tradition, the Bible was looked upon as the crown and the climax of Judaism."

What he particularly misses, as we easily gather, is a distinctive theology for the new orthodoxy. "The historical school," he says, "has never, to my knowledge, offered the world a theological programme of its own. . . . As far as we may gather from vague remarks and hints thrown out now and then, its theological position may perhaps be thus defined :— It is not the mere revealed Bible that is of first importance to the Jew, but the Bible as it repeats itself in history, in other

[1] *Liberal Judaism*, Chapter xviii.

words, as it is interpreted by tradition. . . . Since then the interpretation of the Scripture is mainly a product of changing historical influences, it follows that the centre of authority is actually removed from the Bible and placed in some living body," which he goes on to designate "the collective conscience of Catholic Israel as embodied in the Universal Synagogue."

Schechter does not really quarrel with this view, but he complains that the "collective conscience" has not yet found a "safe and rational solution of our present theological troubles." What these troubles are he does not say precisely, but we may shrewdly suspect that the essence of them is the lack of any particularist concept of God according with modern ideas which could serve as a logical basis for Jewish traditional practice.

Schechter's own contribution to the relief of these troubles was his *magnum opus*, *Aspects of Rabbinic Theology*, published in 1909. The object of this work was to present the theological views of the ancient Rabbis, as found chiefly in their *haggadah*, in an ordered and attractive form.

How much of these views Schechter himself was prepared to accept he does not indicate. But his sympathy with them is obvious, and is apt to communicate itself to the reader. If therefore he did not finally settle the theological problem of the "historical" school, he provided a kind of interim solution for which it might well be grateful to him.

Schechter, like Krochmal before him (*vide supra*, p. 107), could not help noticing that the faith for which he was seeking found its strongest expression in the Chassidim; and this fact led him to regard that much-abused body much more sympathetically than Graetz, who had no words of opprobrium strong enough either for them or for the Cabbalah in general. His earliest published English work was an essay on the Chassidim (translated for him by Claude Montefiore), in which, while admitting their later degeneracy, he laid stress on their original redeeming features. This was a point of view which was new to Jewish students in the West, though it was already familiar to Hebrew writers in Eastern Europe; and it opened up a line of inquiry which was not without its influence on Jewish religious thought.

Schechter came to America at a time when the character of the Jewish community there was being completely transformed by the mass immigration of Jews from Eastern Europe, who brought with them the old-fashioned Judaism of the Ghetto with here and there a leavening of *haskalah*. During the thirteen years that he lived in the country he exercised a profound influence on the rising generation, consisting mostly of the American born and educated children of the immigrants.

He showed them how to harmonize the claims of American citizenship with the intensely Jewish way of life which they had seen, and often learnt to love, in their own homes in their childhood. Under him the Jewish Theological Seminary, which hitherto had been almost unknown, became a powerful influence in American Jewish life. It attracted large numbers of earnest students, and was able to vie with the Hebrew Union College (*vide*, p. 137) in the supply of Rabbis and teachers. These men preached a doctrine intermediate between that of the Reformers and that of the old-fashioned orthodox: that "Judaism is a continuing historical development, that it cannot exist without the *torah*, that it must retain Hebrew as a universal bond, that it can neither break away voluntarily from its past nor remain fixedly in the old ways, neither shed its national character nor be transformed into a secular nationalism." This teaching found a wide response among the younger generation of American Jewry, and created a strong counterblast to the Reform movement which for some years had held undisputed sway.

It even influenced the Reformers themselves, the leaders of whom had always treated Schechter with marked respect; a new statement of the guiding principles of Reform Judaism issued after his death by the Central Conference of American Rabbis was much nearer to tradition than that of the Pittsburgh Platform of fifty years previously.

Schechter's idea that not only the theological and ethical, but also the cultural tradition of Judaism could be successfully fitted into the American way of life was developed by Dr. M. M. Kaplan into a "Program for the Reconstruction of Judaism," which he published in the *Menorah Journal* of New York soon after the first World War. Advocating what he calls a "symbiosis" between Judaism and Americanism, Kaplan affirms that "Israel can maintain its identity within American life and preserve itself as a distinct group if it strengthens and develops its institutions, if it elaborates its hereditary culture and the manifold expressions of its folk-spirit, if it cultivates the Hebrew language and its literary manifestations, if it recognizes Eretz Israel (Jewish Palestine) as its cultural centre." Religion in this scheme would be preserved, more or less in its traditional form, as a "cultural factor."

Such a programme could hardly be expected to have a popular appeal, but it has probably influenced certain leaders of thought and so contributed to the preservation of traditional Judaism in America.

CHAPTER XV

NATIONALIST JUDAISM

THE new forms of Judaism which were developed in Western Europe and America from the time of Mendelssohn onwards were all *religious*—they all took their start from a theology. Those who framed them accepted the principle laid down by Mendelssohn, that the bases of religion (if any) can and should be determined by the human reason without the aid of revelation. But in applying this principle they had all reached the belief that there really was a God, a Creator, and that religion in consequence was a necessity for the human spirit. Certainly they differed considerably in the conceptions of God which they derived from their reason, being strongly influenced by the views current on this subject in their non-Jewish environment.

Thus Mendelssohn, under the influence of the Leibnitz-Wolf school, accepted the deistic view of God as the author of the universe, while Claude Montefiore, under the influence of James Martineau, conceived of God rather as the source of soul and spirit. There were also great differences among the rationalists on the subject of revelation. But even those who narrowed revelation down to a mere psychological phenomenon still clung to the God-idea. For those who rejected the God-idea there was no room in any of the Western forms of Judaism.

Among the East European Jews this was not the case. Here the rationalists, as pointed out above (Chapter viii), were the *maskilim*, men who combined European culture with the habitual use of Hebrew as the literary vehicle for expressing their thoughts. Many of the *maskilim*—perhaps a larger proportion than among the rationalists of the West—abandoned entirely the Jewish religion, both in belief and in practice.

Yet they did not on that account cease to belong to the Jewish community or to take a keen interest in matters Jewish.

A striking example was presented by Osias (Joshua) Schorr (1814–1895), of Brody in Galicia, a friend of Nachman Krochmal. Of an excessively critical disposition, Schorr adopted in an extreme form the rationalistic ideas of the day and rejected Jewish tradition uncompromisingly. Yet for many years he edited a Hebrew magazine called *He-Chalutz* (The Pioneer), which was devoted to Jewish affairs and became an important forum of Jewish opinion. He also strongly supported religious education for the young as the only way of keeping them within the Jewish fold.

Eager as they were to keep abreast of modern thought, many of the *maskilim* were quick to imbibe the scientific theories regarding the origin of the universe and the evolution of man which began to spread about the middle of the century. This naturally meant the end of religion for many of them; and in the sixties and seventies the *maskilim* of Odessa, the great centre of *haskalah*, were notorious for their irreligion. Yet even these remained in the community.

While relaxing the religious bond which had formerly united them to the Jewish people they preserved and strengthened the linguistic bond. They remained devotedly attached to the Hebrew language, which they regarded as the Jewish heritage and the proper vehicle for Jewish self-expression. But the form and tone of that expression were entirely European.

This linguistic bond was hardly sufficient to give them that sense of organic cohesion with their people which alone could satisfy their Jewish feeling. For this purpose some stronger bond was needed, and the *maskilim* could not rest satisfied till they had found it. In this situation it was natural that they should turn to the idea of nationalism which was then spreading over Europe, especially among the smaller peoples. The essence of this idea was that membership of the same nation constituted at least as strong a bond between individuals as membership of the same religion or the same state. Obviously if this idea could be applied to the Jewish people the problem of the *maskilim* would be solved.

Could then the Jews be regarded as a nation? On the

surface they seemed to lack one qualification which might be considered essential—an organic connection with a soil that bore their name. It was primarily this connection which had led many other peoples in Europe in the nineteenth century to realize that they were nations in the full sense of the term—the Spanish, the Germans, the Greeks, the Italians, the Hungarians and now the Balkan peoples. On the other hand, the Jews possessed in abundant measure another asset which had been hardly less important than the soil for awakening national sentiment in the peoples of Europe—a national culture embodied in language, custom and literature.

In the Bible the Jews had a literature which reflected the life they had once lived as a nation on a land of their own, and which kept alive in them with peculiar vividness both the memory of that past life and the hope of its restoration. And in fact by their cultivation of the Hebrew language and their immersion in the study of the Bible—which some of them got to know so well that they were dubbed "walking concordances" —the *maskilim* made up for the lack of a national soil and were able to apply the national idea to the Jews purely in virtue of their national culture.

The writer who gave clearest expression to this Jewish national idea and did most to popularize it was a Lithuanian Jew named Peretz Smolenskin (1842–1885). In his time Smolenskin was the greatest modernizer of the Hebrew language, which he made into a facile instrument for dealing with the topics of the day, both Jewish and general. In 1868 he settled in Vienna, the meeting-ground of conflicting nationalities, where nationalism was so to speak in the air. More strongly than ever in such an environment he realized that he was a Jew by nationality, and that this fact distinguished him sharply from the assimilating Jews of the Vienna community. He could see no future for the Jewish people in assimilation.

On the other hand he could not help observing that national sentiment was giving a new hope to the oppressed subject nationalities of the Ottoman Empire and was nerving them to an effort to throw off their yoke. What was good for them, he reasoned, could not be bad for the Jews.

These views were embodied by Smolenskin in a book—or long essay—which he wrote in Hebrew in 1873 under the title of *Am Olam* (Eternal People). His main point was that the Jews had survived in the past through considering themselves a nation, and this would enable them to survive in the future also. Hence their eyes should be directed to Palestine, as their only real homeland, and the one place where they could hope to be independent both spiritually and materially. Meanwhile they should preserve their connection with Palestine by studying Hebrew and using it to the utmost extent as a living tongue. In this way they would strengthen their national consciousness, which was the first condition for effecting their restoration to their ancient home.

In exhorting the Jews to try to regain Palestine by their own efforts, without waiting to be redeemed by a heaven-sent Messiah, Smolenskin had been anticipated by a German Jew, the well-known Socialist leader Moses Hess (1812–1875). In 1862 Hess had published a book called *Rom und Jerusalem* in which he had suggested the return of the Jews as a nation to Palestine in order to establish there the perfect Socialist state. Hess's work made little impression on the general public, but from internal evidence it would seem that Smolenskin borrowed many ideas from it. There was, however, a fundamental difference between his approach and that of Hess to the question of the Jewish return to Palestine. Hess had advocated it primarily for the sake of humanity at large, but Smolenskin with his much stronger Jewish feelings desired it first and foremost for the sake of the Jews themselves.

The *Am Olam* was widely read in Russia—and not only by *maskilim*—and may be said to have created in Russian Jewry a Jewish national consciousness analogous to the national consciousness of the other peoples of Europe. This consciousness was not in itself incompatible with the religious sentiment, though naturally it flourished most readily in those in whom this sentiment was absent. Its working was at first purely psychological, and it did not for a time lead to any effort to realize the idea of a national restoration.

It was not long, however, before the Jews of Russia were driven by the stress of circumstances to recognize the need of such an effort; and in making it they evolved a new form of Judaism which derived its whole inspiration from the national consciousness.

At the time when Smolenskin wrote his *Am Olam* the Jews in the Russian Empire were still cherishing hopes that they would be granted at least a measure of political rights in Russia. Their watchword was still "emancipation," as it had been since the accession of Alexander II to the throne nearly twenty years before. The idea of a return to Palestine might be tempting in theory, but it was not urgent, as there were prospects of their position in Russia becoming at least tolerable in the near future. But these hopes were entirely dispelled by the assassination in 1880 of Alexander II and the repressive régime of Alexander III which followed. The Jews became regretfully convinced that there was no future for them under the Czarist rule in Russia, and began to look around for a refuge.

The mass of the Jews in Russia at this time were culturally on much the same level as the Jews of Poland had been a hundred years before. Since the introduction of the *haskalah* in the early years of the century there had been no lack of intellectual ferment among them, and this had greatly leavened the mass, but it had not fundamentally altered its character. Various movements of revolt against talmudic Judaism had sprung up, and revolutionary and nihilistic views had found an entry even into the *yeshiboth* (Talmudical colleges) themselves. Nevertheless the bulk of the Russian Jews had continued to regard the Talmud with the greatest reverence and to follow the guidance of the talmudically trained Rabbis.

It was this class which now commenced to emigrate in large numbers to England and America. Here they established in many of the large towns veritable Ghettos where they followed exactly the same way of life as they had done in Russia. They continued to speak Yiddish and to regard the Talmud as the sum and substance of all wisdom. Those who came over in middle age or later for the most part remained to the end impervious to the influence of their non-Jewish environment.

But those who came over younger, and still more the English-born children of the immigrants, were naturally more susceptible. That they should follow in the footsteps of the older generation was not to be expected. Thus in respect of the relations between the older and younger generations,[1] the conditions which prevailed in the German Ghettos in the time of Mendelssohn were reproduced, with the difference that there now existed outside of the Ghetto various forms of Judaism in which the modern spirit found a place. Instead of having to create new forms for themselves, the younger generation was able to choose between those already established. In fact, they brought fresh vigour and a new lease of life to these forms, carrying on in their own way the work which had been commenced by Western Jews—mostly German —in the century preceding.

In this individualistic *sauve qui peut* emigration to England and America the nationally conscious Jews of Russia took little part. They also felt acutely the blow of General Ignatieff's May Laws, but their reaction to it was somewhat different from that of the masses. They drew from it the conclusion that the time had definitely arrived to create a Jewish nation with a homeland of its own, where it would be in no danger either of absorption or of persecution. The case for acquiring such a territory was stated with great force by Leo Pinsker, a well known physician of Odessa, in a German brochure entitled *Autoemancipation*, published in 1884. Pinsker in many ways anticipated the proposals put forward more than a decade later by Theodor Herzl, which led to the creation of the Zionist movement.

Like Herzl he advocated as the basis of his scheme the acquisition by purchase of a territory—not necessarily Palestine—large enough to find room for a substantial number of Jews. In his further development of the project, however, he diverged significantly from Herzl. The latter's approach to the problem was fundamentally philanthropic; his original idea was to obtain money from rich Western Jews who would not themselves become members of his Jewish settlement but who would assist their less fortunate brethren. Pinsker's approach, on the other hand, was essentially nationalistic; his idea was

[1] A vivid description of these relations is given in I. Zangwill's *Children of the Ghetto*, published in 1892.

NATIONALIST JUDAISM 155

that the Jews who provided the money should themselves settle in the territory to be acquired and help to turn it into a national home for their people.

It was this nationalist note in Pinsker's scheme which led to the emergence of a new form of Judaism, through the emphasis laid on it by Pinsker's chief friend and coadjutor, Moses Leb Lilienblum (1843–1910). Like Smolenskin, Lilienblum was a Lithuanian Jew who had made a reputation as a Hebrew writer. After being brought up in the strictest orthodoxy he had early become a *maskil*, and among the *maskilim* had become conspicuous for his hostility to the Talmud and to the Jewish religion in general. He confessed, however, that the loss of religion had left him with nothing but "dismay, emptiness of mind, and confusion of soul."

He now saw an opportunity of filling the aching void in his heart by transforming the Jewish national idea into an ideal which could absorb the whole of his energies. For this purpose, while accepting Pinsker's scheme in broad outline, he insisted on two important modifications. One was that the territory for the Jewish homeland must be no other than Palestine, the land which already possessed for the Jews the associations of a home. The other was that the appeal for support of the new movement should be based primarily on these associations, and should emphasize its idealistic character as a form of service of the Jewish nation.

Jews had gone to Palestine from Russia before Lilienblum from idealistic motives, but those motives had been religious; they had gone because they felt that in the Holy Land they could serve God more devoutly and observe the precepts with better heart. For this service of God Lilienblum now substituted the service of the Jewish nation as the determining motive. For him personally such service became the essence of Judaism, and he derived from it the same satisfaction as the religious Jews derived from the service of God. He thus initiated a new kind of Judaism completely "this-worldly" in character, and therefore more fully in accordance with the prevailing spirit of the age than the most advanced forms of religious Judaism.

Although a writer, Lilienblum was essentially a man of

action, and he sought to realize his new conception of Judaism in practice without stopping to formularize it. He became the secretary—and moving spirit—of a committee which was formed in Odessa to promote Jewish colonization in Palestine, and in that capacity gave a living example of what was meant by service of the Jewish nation. The Committee—which soon established branches in many parts of the world—called themselves *Chovevei Zion* (Lovers of Zion), and their movement *Chibbath Zion* (Love of Zion). The name "Zion" had for Jews both religious and national associations, calling up visions on the one hand of the kingship of the House of David, on the other hand of the Temple Service and the Divine Presence. As used by Lilienblum it was undoubtedly meant to emphasize the nationalist character of the new colonization movement, which was regarded by him as the first step in the transformation of Palestine into a Jewish homeland.

The chief exponent in theory of the Judaism of nationalism was Asher Ginsberg (1856–1927), a close friend and colleague of Lilienblum and one of the leading Hebrew writers of his day. He came from a Chassidic family in Central Russia, and like Lilienblum, after receiving a strictly religious upbringing, he became at an early age a *maskil* and a thoroughgoing rationalist, though he was never so embittered against religious orthodoxy as Lilienblum. He was from the outset an enthusiastic supporter of the *Chibbath Zion* movement, and his writings include a number of essays in which he plays the part of "candid friend" to the movement, seeking to bring it back to the nationalist ideals from which he feared it was departing. All his writings were published under the pseudonym of Achad Ha-am (One of the People), by which he has always been universally known.

In the opening words of the very first of these essays—published in the Hebrew journal *Ha-Melitz* in 1889—Achad Ha-am proclaims the advent of a new form of Judaism which is going to sweep away the old ones. "For many centuries," he says, "the Jewish people, sunk in poverty and degradation, has been sustained by faith and hope in the divine mercy. The present generation has seen the birth of a new and far-reaching idea [the Jewish national idea] which promises to bring down our faith and hope from heaven, and transform both into living and active forces, making our land the goal of hope and our people the anchor of faith."

He goes on to endow this idea with something of the character of a revelation. "Historic ideas of this kind spring forth suddenly, as though of their own accord, when the time is ripe. They at once establish their sway over the minds which respond to them, and from these they spread abroad and make their way through the world. . . . It was in this way that our idea came to birth, without our being able to say who discovered it."

Later in the same essay Achad Ha-am asserts that service of the nation is the original and pure form of Judaism. "All the laws and ordinances of Moses, all the blessings and curses of the Law of Moses have but one unvarying object: the well-being of the nation as a whole in the land of its inheritance. The happiness of the individual is not regarded. The individual Israelite is treated as standing to the people of Israel in the relation of a single limb to the whole body: the actions of the individual have their reward in the good of the community." This relation of the individual to the community he calls the sentiment of national loyalty, completely ignoring the fact that the Bible itself invariably speaks of it as the service of God.

It was only later, according to him, "when the nation's star had almost set," that the well-being of the individual as such, "whether in time or in eternity," came into prominence. In other words, the conception of Judaism as a religion, with the saving of the individual soul as its principal objective, was a kind of temporary aberration forced on the Jewish people by the stress of circumstances, and it was now time to revert to what might be called the archetypal conception of service of the nation as the essence of Judaism.

Up to this point Achad Ha-am was without doubt correctly representing the views of Lilienblum also. But there was an important difference between the two on the question of what was comprised in the service of the Jewish nation. Lilienblum for all his idealism was a complete materialist. His goal was the physical restoration of the Jewish people to their ancient home. This to him was an end in itself, beyond which he did not look. The task which he set himself, and which absorbed all his energies, was to rescue the Jewish people from its age-long homelessness; any ulterior aim had no interest for him.

Achad Ha-am's ideals, unlike Lilienblum's, were spiritual and not material. He could see no value in the return of Israel to his own land unless it was for a spiritual purpose. That purpose was to make the Jewish people once more the representative of the ideals which he found in the prophetical writings of the Old Testament. He noted with deep sorrow that these ideals had lost their grip on the Jewish people in the Diaspora and no longer spurred them on to lofty endeavours.

It was true that the "mission of Israel" in the West set out to win the acceptance by mankind in general of these ideals, but this endeavour was apt to evaporate in pulpit addresses and appeals without making any impact on the hard world of reality. "Jüdische Wissenschaft" was equally ineffective, because it was concerned more with the dead past than with the living present. As for his own fellow-Jews in Russia, the mass of them followed a petrified routine which had lost all the spiritual value it once possessed.

The one place in Achad Ha-am's opinion where the Jews might hope to remedy this state of affairs and give fresh vitality to the prophetic ideals was Palestine, provided they returned there under the proper conditions and in the right spirit. The conditions were more or less those envisaged by Lilienblum, but the spirit was one with which Lilienblum showed little sympathy; and it was over this point that the two friends found themselves constantly in controversy.

Lilienblum was for settling the maximum number of Jews in Palestine who were likely to make good colonists. Achad Ha-am demanded that they should be spiritually qualified also and selected from this point of view. Lilienblum wanted merely a home for the Jewish people; Achad Ha-am wanted what he called a "spiritual centre," where the Jews would make it their object to clothe the prophetic ideals in new forms suitable to modern life and conditions; where they would restore "the dominance of that moral force which was implanted in our people centuries ago, which itself produced the Book, and renewed the spirit of the Book in each successive period, according to its own needs."[1] This task he considered impossible of fulfilment in the Diaspora, but he apparently imagined that the air of Palestine would in some way furnish Jews of the right type with the wisdom needed to perform it.

Like Montefiore's Liberal Judaism, Achad Ha-am's Spiritual Zionism is completely independent of Jewish law. While he had the greatest admiration for Moses as a prophet, he had no use at all for Moses as a lawgiver. But he differed from Montefiore in regarding Moses as a Jewish national hero, if only a legendary one. The prophet in his eyes represented the ideal Jewish character as evolved in the national consciousness, and Moses personified the prophet in his most complete form. In its picture of Moses, he says, the Jewish people represented itself; and he quotes with approval a saying of the Cabbalists that "Moses is reincarnated in every age." In the Jewish nationalist movement he saw some beginning of "a reincarnation of Moses," and for that reason he supported it.

Achad Ha-am's form of Judaism is commonly called "spiritual Zionism," a term which he himself never used, but which correctly marks the fact that his conception of "Zion" embraced first and foremost the spiritual elements associated with the name. It presented many striking points of contact with the Liberal Judaism of Claude Montefiore which he criticized so severely. Like Montefiore, Achad Ha-am had an unbounded admiration for the Hebrew prophets and regarded the ideals which they enunciated as the highest goal of human, and particularly Jewish, endeavour. Like him too he saw in the observance of the Jewish law a hindrance rather than an aid to the pursuit of these ideals at the present day. Also like Montefiore he was not satisfied with a private and individual cultivation of them, but desired to see them fostered by some great and collective effort which would impress the world.

But while both were aiming at the same goal they sought to reach it by diametrically opposite paths. For Montefiore belief in God was a *sine qua non* of Judaism, for Achad Ha-am it was an irrelevance. Montefiore made his starting point the

[1] Essay on "The Transvaluation of Values."

religious sentiment and reached his spiritual values by way of the emotions; Achad Ha-am made the national sentiment his starting-point and reached his spiritual values by way of the intellect. For Montefiore's purpose the Jews had to be a religious community only and not a nation, for Achad Ha-am's they had to be a nation only and not a religious community. Montefiore's method involved the final disintegration of the Jewish people, Achad Ha-am's its reintegration in its ancient vigour.

The form of Judaism propounded by Lilienblum and Achad Ha-am had its roots in Russia and grew out of the combination by the *maskilim* of irreligion with strong Jewish feeling. But by its nature it was meant to be transplanted to Palestine and to find there its centre. When Achad Ha-am commenced writing the prospect of such a development seemed remote.

The stream of Jewish colonists was for years very thin, and only a small proportion of them went to Palestine purely for the nationalistic reasons desired by Achad Ha-am. But this proportion included the bulk of one class which was of cardinal importance for the future of Judaism in the country—the teachers. Most of these were ardent disciples of Achad Ha-am, and in Palestine they found free scope for their energies and were able to implant their own ideas of religion and nationality in a large section of the rising generation.

Concurrently the nationalist idea obtained a firmer hold of the Jewish youth in East Europe, and inspired many of them of both sexes to train themselves systematically for carrying out pioneer work in Palestine. These were known as *chalutzim* (pioneers), and numbers of them in due course went to Palestine and formed there communal settlements in which they undertook the hardest and most dangerous work involved in reclaiming the soil. Later, when Britain became the mandatory Power of Palestine, the *chalutz* movement spread to the West also.

Through the influx of the *chalutzim* and the growth of a new Hebrew-speaking generation trained in the ideas of Achad Ha-am, Palestine since the war of 1914–1918 has become the home of a type of Jew to which the service of the Jewish nation is the normal expression of Judaism, just as the service of God was to previous generations. It is natural that this type

NATIONALIST JUDAISM 161

should have tended to become more representative than any other of Judaism in the country. For it is this type which is best qualified to devote itself whole-heartedly to the cause of the Jewish national revival in Palestine, which is so intimately bound up with the problem of Jewish survival in general. Its growth too has been fostered by the chief educational establishment in the country, the Hebrew University in Jerusalem, founded in 1925, which similarly aims at promoting the Jewish national revival, and not the Jewish religion in any shape or form.

In their attitude to religion this type differs somewhat from the old Russian *maskilim*, among whom the Judaism of nationalism originated. They are not so much irreligious as a-religious. They regard religion not so much with antipathy as with indifference, as something which lies outside their lives and belongs to another age. The idea of the Jewish national revival is sufficient to fill their mental horizon, and the service of the Jewish nation to engage all their energies. They apply to the Jewish religion the same test as they would apply to anything else—will it assist the Jewish national revival? Actually they find many elements of national value in the Jewish ceremonial; thus they keep the Sabbath as the weekly day of rest and the Jewish festivals as national holidays.

Hence a Jew who desires to observe the Jewish ceremonial can perhaps do so more easily in Palestine than in any other country; and this itself is a reason why many religious Jews are anxious to settle there.

After the close of the Second World War the religious elements in the Jewish people began to support much more actively the political strivings of the nationalists, investing them with something of the character of a messianic movement. The fruit of this collaboration was the establishment in 1948 of a Jewish state in Palestine. This event would seem on the face of it to constitute a challenge to the Messianic hope of the Jewish religion, which has always linked the national restoration with the advent of a heaven-sent deliverer of the House of David. Nor does the character of the present state at all correspond with the theocracy which is envisaged in the Messianic hope.

Nevertheless there is a strong disposition among at any

L

rate the older generation of orthodox Jews to see in the new state at least a partial fulfilment of the age-long prayers of the Jewish people, and a triumphant if not yet final justification of their Jewish faith. For them recent events in Palestine are a religious as well as a national tonic.

The future of Judaism, however, lies with the younger generation; and whether these can be induced to see the matter in the same light is highly problematical. The decisive factor in this issue will probably be the line taken by the younger Jews in Palestine; and these are inclined to interpret history, including Jewish history, in Nietzschian, or even Marxian rather than in Biblical terms. That this tendency should be reversed does not seem likely; yet it is by no means impossible.

The environment in which the younger Jews of the new Israel state find themselves tends naturally to make them great readers of the Hebrew Scriptures, often to the exclusion of all other reading. No doubt the chief purpose of this reading is at present to keep alive and stimulate the national sentiment. But in the Bible itself the national sentiment is inextricably interwoven with the religious, and it is not easy for the Jewish reader to imbibe the one while eschewing the other. Just as in the nineteenth century the religiously-trained *maskilim* in Russia found in the Bible the seed of a new Jewish nationalism (*vide supra*, p. 151), so it is conceivable that the nationalistically-trained Jews in Palestine will find in it the seed of a new Jewish God-idea. In this possibility lies certainly the best, perhaps the only hope of a Jewish religious revival.

GLOSSARY

ABODAH: The Temple service
CHAKHAM: An alternative title for Rabbi
CHASSIDIM: The followers of Israel Baalshem
GEMARA: The glosses on the Mishnah compiled at the end of the fourth and fifth centuries
HAGGADAH: The non-legal part of the Talmud
HALAKHAH: The legal part of the Talmud
MASKIL (plu. Maskilim): An Hebraic rationalist
MIDRASH: The Rabbinic exposition of the Scriptures
MISHNAH: The code of Jewish customary law compiled by R. Judah ha-Nasi
MITZVAH (plu. Mitzvoth): A religious precept or duty
ORAL LAW: The legislation contained in the Talmud
ORTHODOXY: The rule of conduct prescribed in the Shulchan Arukh
RABBI: A Jewish religious teacher
SCRIBES: The successors of Ezra as the chief Jewish religious authority
SHULCHAN ARUKH: The handbook of Jewish religious practice compiled by Joseph Caro
TALMID CHAKHAM (plu. Talmide Chakhamim): A Talmudical student or scholar
TALMUD: The combination of the Mishnah with the Gemara
TORAH: Jewish religious doctrine based on the Sinaitic revelation
WRITTEN LAW: The legislation contained in the Pentateuch

Note: In the transliteration of Hebrew words ch represents a soft guttural as in the German "ich", and kha hard guttural as in the Scotch "loch".

BIBLIOGRAPHY

The following works (in English) may be useful for those who desire to pursue further subjects touched on in the foregoing pages.

INTRODUCTION
T. Herford, *Pharisaism*.

CHAPTER I
Encyclopedia Biblica, art. Samaritans.
Jewish Encyclopedia, artt. Samaritans, Canon, Scribes.

CHAPTER II
Schürer, *History of the Jews*, Vol. II.
Josephus, *Antiquities*, XVIII.
Jewish Encyclopedia, artt. Pharisees, Sadducees.

CHAPTER III
G. F. Moore, *Judaism in the first century of the Christian Era*, Vol. II.
Graetz, *History of the Jews*,[1] Vol. II, ch. VI.
D. Castelli, Future Life in Rabbinic Literature, in *Jewish Quarterly Review*, 1889.
W. Hirsch, *Rabbinical Doctrine of the Soul* (London, 1947).
Jewish Encyclopedia, artt. Halachah, Hagadah, Midrash.
A. Cohen, *Everyman's Talmud*.
H. Danby, *Translation of the Mishnah* (Oxford, 1933).

CHAPTER IV
Graetz, *History*, Vol. III, ch. V.

---

[1] The translation referred to is that of Bella Loewy and Israel Abrahams in five volumes. The original German is much fuller. A fuller translation in six volumes was also issued by the Jewish Publication Society of America in 1941, but it is not easily procurable in England.

Jewish Encyclopedia, artt. Karaites, Anan, Benjamin Nahawendi, Saadiah, Spain.

Saadiah Studies (Manchester, 1943).

CHAPTER V

Graetz, *History*, Vol. III, ch. XV.
Leon Roth, *Maimonides* (London, 1949).
Jewish Encyclopedia, art. Maimonides.

CHAPTER VI

Graetz, *History*, Vol. III, ch. XV; Vol. V, ch. IV.
Jewish Encyclopedia, artt. I. Luria, Sabbatai Zevi, Donmeh, J. Frank.
E. Müller, *History of the Cabbalah* (London, 1948).

CHAPTER VII

Jewish Encyclopedia, artt. Chassidim, Israel Baalshem, Elijah Vilna, Baer of Meseritz.
S. Shechter, The Chassidim, and Elijah Wilner (in *Essays on Judaism*).
I. Zangwill, The Master of the Name (in *Dreamers of the Ghetto*).

CHAPTER VIII

Graetz, *History*, Vol. V, ch. VIII.
Jewish Encyclopedia, artt. Mendelssohn, Wessely.
J. Heller, *Pioneers of Haskalah* (London, 1946).

CHAPTER IX

J. Klausner, *History of Modern Hebrew Literature* (tr. Danby, London, 1932).
Jewish Encyclopedia, artt, Wessely, Measfim.
S. Schechter, Nachman Krochmal (in *Essays on Judaism*).
I. Zangwill, Nathan the Wise and Solomon the Fool (in *Dreamers of the Ghetto*).
J. Heller, *Rapaport, Krochmal and S.D. Luzzatto*.

CHAPTER X

Graetz, *History*, Vol. V, ch. XII.
Jewish Encyclopedia, artt. Furtado, Sinzheim, Emancipation, Jacobsohn.

BIBLIOGRAPHY 167

I. Zangwill, From A Mattress Grave (in *Dreamers of the Ghetto*).

CHAPTER XI

Graetz, *History*, Vol. V, ch. XV.
Jewish Encyclopedia, artt. Bernays, Mannheimer, Sachs, Zunz, S. D. Luzzatto, S. R. Hirsch.
S. R. Hirsch. *The Nineteen Letters of Ben Uziel* (translated by B. Drachman, New York, 1899).
M. Joseph, *Judaism as Creed and Life*.
D. Philipson, *The Reform Movement in Judaism* (Philadelphia, 1944).

CHAPTER XII

Jewish Encyclopedia, artt. Geiger, Holdheim, Reform.
I. Ritter, Samuel Holdheim (in *Jewish Quarterly Review*, 1889).
I. Elbogen, *A Century of Jewish Life* (New York, 1933).

CHAPTER XIII

Jewish Encyclopedia, artt. Reform, I. M. Wise.
K. Kohler, *Jewish Theology*.
C. Montefiore, *Liberal Judaism*.

CHAPTER XIV

Jewish Encyclopedia, artt. Frankel, Graetz.
N. Bentwich, *Solomon Schechter* (Philadelphia, 1938).

CHAPTER XV

J. Klausner, *History of Modern Jewish Literature*.
L. Simon, *Moses Leb Lilienblum* (Cambridge, 1912).
Achad Ha-am, *Selected Essays*, translated by L. Simon.
J. Heller, *The Zionist Idea* (London, 1947).

INDEX

INDEX

ABBA MARI, 66
Abrahamism, 109
Abu Isa, 47
Abulafia, Meir, 61, 63
Achad Ha'am, 156, 157, 158, 159, 160
Ada (Rabbi), 23
Adler, N. M., 116
Adret, Solomon ben, 66
Akiba (Rabbi), 22
Alconstantin, Bachiel, 63
Alexander II of Russia, 153
Alexander III of Russia, 153
Alfachar, Jehudah, 63
Alsace, 112, 115
Am Olam, 152
America, 133, 154
American Jews, 147
American Rabbis, 134, 138
Amsterdam, 74
Amulets, 75
Anan, 47, 48, 49
Apocalyptic Works, 32
Arabic, 51, 54, 55, 59
Arabic Literature, 89
Arabic Period, 11, 53, 89
Anthropomorphism, 50
Aragon, 63, 64
Asheri, 66
Aspects of Rabbinic Theology, 146
Assimilation, 115, 130, 134
Assumptio Mosis, 32
Atticism, 109
Auto-emancipation, 154
Austria, 98

BAALSHEM, ISRAEL, 78, 79, 82
Bachya ibn Pakuda, 59

Ban, 62, 84
Bar Cochba, 41
Beer, B. I., 112, 114
Beliefs and Opinions, 55, 59
Ben Sira, 23
Benjamin Nahawendi, 50
Ber of Meseritz, 79, 81
Berlin, 90, 91
Berlin Temple, 132
Bernays, I., 124
Beth Yehudah, 106
Bezières, 62
Bibelscher Orient, 123, 124
Bible, 127, 136, 145, 151, 162. See also "Scriptures"
Bible Translations, 52, 94
Biur, 101, 123
Bordeaux, 112
Breslau Seminary, 143
Breslau Conference, 134
Bresselau, M., 101
Book of Jubilees, 32
Brunswick Conference, 131

CABBALAH, 68, 69, 72, 146. See also "Zohar"
Canon (Scriptural), 22, 23
Carpathians, 78
Caro, J., 72
Chabad, 83
Chakham, 124
Chakhamim, 33
Chassidim, 80, 82, 83, 84, 103, 146
Chalutzim, 160
Chelebi, R. J., 74
Chivi ha-Balchi, 58
Chovevei Zion, 156
Chozari, 59
Church, Christian, 11

INDEX

Cincinnatti, 135
Cleveland, 131
Circumcision, 131
Citizenship, 112, 113, 118
Conferences, Rabbinical, 131, 132, 135, 136, 137, 147
Cordoveiro, M., 72
Council of Notables, 113
Creeds, 55
Crimea, 57
Culture, 89, 123
Custom, 28

DAVID BEN SAUL, 62, 64
"Day of the Lord," 30
Dessau, 91
Dietary Laws, 131
Dominicans, 64, 65
Dönmeh, 76
Dositheus, 25
Dubno, S., 101
Duties of the Heart, 59

EAST EUROPE, 76
Education, 97, 98, 106
Egypt, 74
Eibeschütz, J., 75
Einhorn, D., 138
Eleazar ben Jacob (Rabbi), 41
Elijah Vilna, 83, 104
Emancipation, 112, 113, 118, 153
Emden, J., 75
Emigration, 153
En Sof, 69
Encyclopédie, 107
England, 90, 154
English Jews, 120
"Enlightenment," 93, 104, 107
Enoch, Book of 32
Eschatology, 10, 32
Essenes, 38, 39
Euchel, I., 101
Europeanising, 91, 93
Exegesis, 54
Exilarch, 48

Ezra the Priest, 9, 17, 26
Ezra ben Solomon, 68

FAITH AND REASON, 108
Forbidden Foods, 122
France, 90, 113
Frank, Jacob, 76
Frankel, Z., 142, 143
Frankfort Conference, 132
Frankfort Pietists, 126
Franz Joseph II, 98
Friedländer, D., 97, 119
Furtado, A., 113, 114
Future World, 36

GALICIA, 103
Gan Eden, 36
Gans, E., 119
Gaonim, 47, 48
Gehinnom, 36
Gemara, 43
Gerizim, Mt., 20, 24
German, 94, 100, 102, 106
Germany, 65, 90, 98, 117, 118
Geiger, A., 128, 129, 130, 132, 133, 137, 142, 143
Gerona, 68
Ghetto, 90, 93, 154
Ginsberg, A., v. Achad Ha'am
Gnostics, 44, 69
Graetz, H., 143, 144
Greek Philosophy, 58
Gottesdienstliche Vorträge der Juden, 123
Guide of the Perplexed, 59, 61, 62, 64, 66
Guide of the Perplexed of the Age, 108

HAGADAH, 44, 45, 60, 70
Halakhah, 33, 60
Hamburg, 118, 119, 120, 124, 125
Hamelitz, 156
Haskalah, 84, 104, 106, 107, 123, 153
Hasmoneans, 27
Hebraism, 10, 54

INDEX

Hebrew, 92, 100, 106, 125, 136, 150
Hebrew University, 161
Hebrew Union College, 137, 147
Hechalutz, 150
Heine H., 119
Herschell, S., 116
Hess, M., 152
Herzl, T., 154
Hillel (Rabbi), 34, 35
Hillel of Verona, 65
Hirsch, S. R., 125, 141, 144
High Priest, 26, 41
Historical School, 142, 143, 145, 146
Hizzuk Emunah, 56
Hofjuden, 90
Holdheim, S., 130, 131, 132, 144
Holiness, 121, 122, 136
Holland, 90
Hohenzollern, 90
Holy Spirit, 18

IBN DAUD, A., 59
Ibn Ezra, A., 54
Ibn Gabirol, S., 54
Ibn Tibbon, Jacob, v. Profatius
Ibn Tibbon, S., 61
Immortality of the Soul, 35, 136
Inspiration, 9
Intercessor, 40
Israel ben Eleazar Baalshem, v. Baalshem
Israel the Blind, 68
Italy, 67, 92
Itzig, D., 98

JACOBSOHN, I., 117, 119
James of Aragon, 64
Jedaiah Bedaresi, 67
Jehudah Halevi, 54, 59
Jerusalem, 20
Jerusalem, 94
Jesus, 39, 40, 80
Jerome, Prince, 118
Jew-Hatred, 119

Jewish Culture, 123
Jewish History, 128, 129
Jewish Law, 114
Jewish Nation, 143
Jewish People, 9, 10, 108
Jewish Persuasion, 114, 116
Jewish Religion, 9, 53
Jewish Religious Union, 140
Jewish State, 161
Jewish Theological Seminary, 145, 147
Jewish Tradition, 109, 141, 145
Jews of Germany, 117, 118
Jews of Poland, 102, 105
John the Baptist, 39
John Hyrcanus, 24
Jonah b. Abraham (Gerondi), 62, 64, 65
Jonathan (Rabbi), 44
Jubilees, Book of, 32
Judaism, 9, 12, 13, 114, 140
Judah Ha-nasi, 35
Judeans, 17
Judeo-Arabic Culture, 53, 54
Jüdische Wissenschaft, 127, 158
Jurisprudence, 10

KAPLAN, M. M., 147
Kara, 49
Karaism, 51, 56
Karaites, 49, 50, 56, 57, 121
Kavvanah, 72
Kimchi, D., 62
Kohler, K., 137
Königsberg, 90, 101
Krochmal, N., 107, 128, 146

LAST JUDGMENT, 30
Legislation, Mosaic, 26, 96
Lessing, E., 93, 124
Levitical Purity, 28, 31, 50
Liberal Judaism, 140, 141, 159
Liberal Synagogue, 140
Lilienblum, M. L., 155, 156, 157, 158
Lilienthal, D., 106

INDEX

Lithuania, 57, 83
Lithuanian Rabbis, 83
Lofty Faith, 59
Luria, I., 72
Lurian Cabbalah, 72, 73
Lunel, 61, 62
Luzzatto, M. C., 92
Luzzatto, S. D., 109, 116, 125

MAIMONIDES, 54, 58, 59, 60, 64, 68
Maimuni, David, 65, 66
Makharites, 50
Manasseh, 19
Mannheimer, I., 125, 142, 144
Marks, D. W., 121
Martineau, J., 141, 149
Maskilim, 84, 103, 149, 150, 160, 161
May Laws, 154
Meassef, 102
Mekilta, 33
Mendel of Vitebsk, 83
Mendelssohn, M., 91, 93, 100, 101, 106, 124, 129, 149
Menorah Journal, 147
Messiah, 38, 39, 47, 77, 135, 152
Messianic Hope, 115, 161
Midrash, 35, 45, 48, 55
Mikra, 19, 21, 22, 48
Minim, 44
Mishnah, 35, 49, 142
Mishneh Torah, 55
Mission of Israel, 138, 140, 141, 158
Mitzvah, 41, 42, 126
Mixed Marriages, 113
Modernism, 12
Monotheism, 129
Montefiore, C., 139, 145, 149, 159, 160
Montpellier, 62, 64, 67
Moser, M., 119
Moses, 159
Moses de Leon, 71
Mutazilites, 50

Mysticism, 10. See also "Cabbalah"

NACHMANIDES, 63, 69
Napoleon, 113, 114, 115
Narbonne, 62
Nathan Ghazzati, 74
National Assembly (French), 112
National Culture, 151
Nationalism, 150, 152
Nazarenes, 40
Nehemiah, 18
Neo-orthodoxy, 126
Neo-Platonists, 69
Nieto, D., 92
Non-Jewish Learning, 92
Northern France, 63
Northern Kingdom (Israel), 20
Notables, Council of, 113

ODESSA, 150, 156
Occultism, 73
Oral Law, 29, 30, 34, 35
Organ, 118
Orthodox, 132, 162
Orthodoxy, 56, 125

PALESTINE, 13, 152, 155
Paraclete, 42
Paris, 64, 65, 112
Pentateuch, 9, 17, 18, 138
Perushim, 28
Peter, 40
Petit, S., 65
Pharisees, 27, 30, 32, 35, 36, 38, 40, 47
Philadelphia Conference, 135
Pittsburg Conference, 135
Podolia, 79
Poland, 90
Polish Rabbis, 79
Progress, 128
Profatius (Profiat Duran), 66, 67
Provence, 61, 62
Practical Cabbalah, 73

INDEX

Prussian Government, 133
Prayer-book (Reform), 125
Pumbeditha, 47

RABBANITES, 50
Rabbinic Judaism, 13
Rabbinism, 37
Rabbis, 10, 12, 34, 37, 43, 45, 49, 72, 78, 95
Rabbis, Modern, 114, 115, 117
Radunitz, 135
Rapaport, S., 128
Rashi, 54
Rebbe, 82
Reform Movement, 118, 119, 120, 121, 122
Reform, Ultra, 131, 132
Reform-Tempel-Verein, 118
Research, 127
Resurrection, 30, 36, 61, 136
Religious Conflicts, 10
Revelation, 9, 68, 157
Riesser, G., 12, 115, 120
Rights of Man, 112
Righteousness, 121
Righteousness and Truth, 95
Russia, 57, 115, 153

SAADIAH, 51 sqq., 55, 59, 65
Sabbath, 49
Sabbatai Zevi, 73 sq.
Sabbatian Movement, 74
Sachs, M., 125, 144
Sadducees, 27, 28, 29, 35, 36, 38, 40, 47
Safed, 72
Salomon, G., 119
Salonica, 74
Salvation, 41
Samaritans, 17, 19, 20, 24, 47
Samuel b. Nachman (Rabbi), 44
Sanhedrin (French), 114, 115, 131
Sasportas, J., 74
Saul of Tarsus, 40
Schechter, S., 145, 146, 147
Schorr, O., 150

Scriptures, 9, 48, 49, 52, 53. See also "Bible"
Scribes, 18, 21, 22, 28, 35
Seesen, 118
Sefer ha-Mitzvoth, 48
Sefiroth, 69
Sermon, 118, 128
Service, 155
Shekinah, 31
Shiites, 48
Sephardim, 84
Shammai, 34, 35
Shma, 46
Shneur Zalman, 83, 84
Shulchan Arukh, 56, 96
Sifra, 33
Sifre, 33
Simon the Just, 27
Simon ben Yochai, 70
Sinzheim, A., 113, 114
Smolenskin, P., 151
Smyrna, 74
Solomon b. Abraham, 61, 62, 64
Song of Songs, 22
Soul, 36, 69
Sources of Torah, 9
Spain, 53, 62
Spiritual Zionism, 159
Spirituality, 10
Studies in Judaism, 145
Symbiosis, 148
Sura, 47

TAHEB, 25
Taku, M., 65
Talmid Chakham, 36, 96
Talmud, 9, 10, 26, 43, 47, 60, 61, 68, 71, 76, 96, 97, 110, 120
Temple Service, 26, 27, 41
Temple (Reform), 118
Testaments of Twelve Patriarchs, 32
Tetragrammaton, 69, 73, 74
Teudah be-Yisroel, 105
Theology, 129, 130, 144, 145, 149
Toleranzedikt, 98
Torah, 9, 10, 11, 12, 21, 29, 82, 89, 137

Troki, I., 56
Tzaddik, 78
Tzaddikism, 81, 84

UNION OF AMERICAN CONGREGATIONS, 134, 143
Union Prayer Book, 137
United States, 112
Urschrift und Uebersetzungen der Bibel, 130

VEREIN FÜR CULTUR, 119
Verein der Reformfreunde, 131
Vienna, 151
Voltaire, 56, 107

WALLACHIA, 79
Wessely, H., 98, 100, 101

West London Synagogue, 121, 139
Westphalia, 118
Wise, I. M., 134, 135, 137
Words of Reason and Truth, 98
Written Law, 29, 121
Ways of the Mishnah, 142

YIDDISH, 90, 94, 102, 113

ZADOKITES, 27
Zekuth Aboth, 42
Zeitschrift für Jüdische Theologie, 130
Zohar, 10, 70, 71, 74, 75
Zunz, L., 108, 119, 123, 128, 142

For Product Safety Concerns and Information please contact our EU
representative GPSR@taylorandfrancis.com
Taylor & Francis Verlag GmbH, Kaufingerstraße 24, 80331 München, Germany

www.ingramcontent.com/pod-product-compliance
Lightning Source LLC
Chambersburg PA
CBHW061449300426
44114CB00014B/1902